Monkeys & Dinosaurs: Cinema as High Art, Vol. 1

Mr. Satanism

Published by Inept Concepts, 2015.

MONKEYS & DINOSAURS: CINEMA AS HIGH ART, VOL. 1

First edition. August 27, 2015.

Copyright © 2015 Mr. Satanism.

ISBN: 979-8227560605

Written by Mr. Satanism.

Introduction

"In the evolutionary development of our planet, human beings and dinosaurs are separated by millions and millions of years. They never walked the earth at the same time." -Some Tool

Leave it to science to ruin everything. Yes it's true that humans and dinosaurs never lived at the same time, but wouldn't it be so much cooler if they did? Just like it would be cooler if lightsabers were in any way practical, or if Taylor Swift was sitting on my lap right now, bouncing up and down as I wrote this. Also she would be dressed as a sexy skunk, for reasons which are really none of your business. But this is why we have movies (and poorly-researched books): so that the impossible can become a reality. Whether the focus is on a Great White Butthole type jonesing to bag the last remaining T. rex, a Brontosaurus hitting the town and busting shit up like a 20-ton sailor on shore leave, or hot, suspiciously-hairless cave chicks losing their tops as they flee from a Dicklodocus in terror, dinosaurs have been a popular subject for movies ever since special effects experts (wrongly) determined that they could be realistically brought to the screen. As for monkey movies, well, there are only two truly great monkey movies: the original *King Kong* (1933), and the time you were bored and watched the original *King Kong* again. But, like cross-dressing and farting, Hollywood can't seem to get enough of monkeys, on the mutually exclusive assumptions that they're both funny and scary, when they're really just smelly and annoying. Of course, the same can be said for dogs, and Julia Roberts, and there's no shortage of movies featuring either of them either. In short, monkey movies suck. But you'll see.

Okay, that's plenty of introduction for a book with a title as self-explanatory as "Monkeys & Dinosaurs". Just read it already.

(**Important Note:** While compiling this guide, I went on the assumption that every Dinosaur Island featured in the following movies is the same place, because that has a certain Wold Newton appeal to it and besides, how many different ones can there be? Sure, it apparently explodes and/or sinks with astonishing regularity, but to paraphrase Mark Twain "The reports of my demise, and the demise of all the dinosaurs inhabiting me, are greatly exaggerated." Frankly I think the Dinosaur Island tourist board just likes to *pretend* that it's been destroyed every few years as a cynical ploy to periodically renew interest, thereby boosting the local economy. That sounds *just like* something they'd do.)

After Dusk They Come

(2009)

Directed by Jorg Ihle

And again in the morning, if they're lucky. Ha ha! *Firefly*'s Kaylee (yum), her homo-ish boyfriend, and three disposable schmucks are shipwrecked on an island inhabited by them-eating monsters. Okay, so this flick isn't exactly mapping out uncharted territory here, but I gotta tell ya, the first half really works. The effect is diminished considerably when we learn that the culprits are killer apes though, because in the grand scheme of things apes just aren't that scary, even when they're smart enough to rig semi-complicated snare traps and have developed a taste for human flesh. Actually, the "apes" we're dealing with here are more akin to ape-*men,* but the difference is negligible unless you're a fundamentalist Christian and if you are trust me, nobody wants to hear about it. Anyway, they pretty much lost me after the ape-men reveal because let's face it, ape-men are basically cavemen and if cavemen were in any way formidable, there would still be some of them around. People die, and some man meat is eaten (heh), but this movie doesn't really linger over the details, so if you're here for the gore you'll probably be disappointed. And would it hurt Kaylee to go topless once in a while by which I mean all the time? Speaking of Kaylee, the expression on her face when one of the ape-men finally corners her only to inexplicably let her go is **priceless**. She looks for all the world like she's thinking "They killed and ate *everyone else* but *I'm* not even good enough to *rape?* Well *fuck you,* ape-men."

Age of Dinosaurs

(2013)

Directed by Joseph J. Lawson

I have no idea what they're trying to prove with the experiment that opens this movie, unless it's that dinosaurs will eat Japanese people, and we already knew that. Whatever the deal, the dinosaurs in question are soon on the loose, although initially they are contained by emergency personnel in a single building, with one of their own on the inside. (It's *Die Hard* with dinosaurs!) (I just made a studio exec ejaculate.). Soon enough though they break out into the surrounding city to engage in various set-pieces: eating cops, invading the mall, and chasing cars down busy streets while disinterested bystanders go about their business like nothing is happening since they obviously can't see the cheesy cartoon effects that will be added later. If I sound dismissive here, that's only because my natural setting is "dick". This is actually a fun movie: the dinosaurs look surprisingly not-awful, there's plenty of carnage, the main guy's daughter is pretty choice (some nice baby-birthin' hips on this one), and an acceptable number of people are scarfed down before it's all over. Frankly I think they also should've included a few graphic, nightmare-inducing gore-mutilations and maybe some tits, but dinosaur movies tend to appeal to children and no one wants children to see tits, so what can you do? As it stands, on a scale of 1 to 10,

I give *Age of Dinosaurs* a solid 8. Oh, and if the opportunity ever presents itself, the actress playing the daughter will be getting a solid 8 from me as well. If you're reading this, toots, I'm on the Facebook.

Alligator X

(2010)

Directed by Amir Valinia

Depending on context, "X" can mean a number of different things. In movie titles, it's often pretentious for the number 10, but it can also indicate "an unknown factor", like in the *X-Men* movies, where the unknown factor is "Why do they keep making these terrible *X-Men* movies?" Well, we know that the monster in this movie is an alligator, and this isn't Part 10, so what the fuck is *this* X for? It's a mystery. Maybe the alligator's name is "Xavier", and "X" is what they call him for short? I'm just gonna go with that.

Actually, to look at Xavier he isn't an alligator at all: he's a mosasaur, a ruthless prehistoric dickbag who, according to the Internet, is the ancestor of the snake. I'm not sure if this was the moviemakers' original intent or if the people who designed the cartoon effects just took their own initiative, but either way I'd say that makes this more of a dinosaur movie than an alligator movie. Rest assured, a class-action lawsuit has already been filed on your behalf. (If we win, you get a nickel!) Complicating the matter further, the scientist who created the mosasaur says that it's a *plesiosaur*, which may or may not be the same thing, although an off-brand amalgamation of several species isn't too surprising seeing as our mad doctor's budget-conscious backwoods take on the

Jurassic Park method of creating dinosaurs is pretty similar to your neighbor's procedure for cooking up meth. At any rate, beyond the challenge of figuring out what the hell Xavier is supposed to be and/or what the moviemakers were thinking, there's not much to hold one's interest here. It's boring, the acting is especially pitiful, and the story mainly consists of talking and rednecks chasing each other around. Even when an entire building is destroyed in one scene – the high point of most monster movies – it's such a ramshackle dump that you can easily imagine the county giving the production a tax break *to* destroy it, thus saving them the trouble. As for what inspired our mad scientist to perpetrate this wild scheme, well, apparently he needed the mosasaur to scare people off so that he could take possession of the surrounding real estate and have room to make more mosasaurs! Like a Möbius strip of stupid, this guy's logic.

Altered States

(1980)

Directed by Ken Russell

With a heavy-handed, drug-friendly title like "Altered States" it's clear that this movie wants so desperately to be perceived as trippy that the only sensible approach is to watch it while perfectly straight, and then ruthlessly mock its overall incomprehensibility. That's right, bucking the established status quo can work both ways, assholes.

So, our main guy is a brilliant, awkward, unconventional research scientist who dabbles in esoteric fields AND is pimp enough to bone an attractive redhead hours after meeting her. Clearly this cat doesn't really exist, which is the first surreal touch of many. Currently our boy is studying the unconscious mind and its ability to plug into flakey hippie bullshit, so he's spending a lot of time inside a sensory-deprivation chamber, which, in reality, might, at worst, make him hallucinate and/or develop pruney fingers. But this is a movie, so when he decides to throw some shrooms into the mix he somehow turns himself into an ape man! And despite all the metaphysical evolutionary-regression genetic-memory fiddlecock on display that really is the primary narrative thrust of this story. Sure, on a deeper level this movie raises any number of big questions, like:

10

How many eyes does a goat need, anyway?

Holy shit, are they watching *Exorcist II* on the television? (They weren't.)

Can we see that chick's tits again?

Who knew that Dan Fielding from *Night Court* was in this movie?

Is it still primordial soup if it has beans in it?

and

Does Charles Haid have any other settings besides "annoying"?

But at the end of the day our main cat is no different from any number of 1940s-era mad doctors who preceded him: he cornholed science with a theory straight out of a comic book, and now he's a goddamned ape man. And, hilariously, the ch-ch-ch-changes don't end there: after some more psychedelic horseshit, including a whirlpool of white liquid that floods the entire lab (I hope that's supposed to be milk), our main guy transmogrifies again, this time into some sort of lumpy mutant. The antidote? Hitting things! (See, ladies? It works.) His girl, meanwhile, has been transformed into magma, but she's quickly cured via the power of *love,* at which point our story ends. And not a moment too soon, because fuck Ken Russell and his sappy-ass, Care Bears bullshit.

A*P*E

(1976)

Directed by Paul Leder

Depicting an island full of dinosaurs is expensive, so this *King Kong* ripoff picks up after they've already captured the giant ape. The ape soon escA*P*Es, jumps ship, and ~~manhandles~~ ape-handles a giant shark (played by a dead shark, so don't get your hopes up for a tussle of biblical proportions or anything) before wading ashore to bust shit up while a handful of extras flee with their valises. And we're not even ten minutes in yet! A*P*E hurls some barrels around à la Donkey Kong, disrupts a kung fu movie shoot (this flick goes down in Asia, so of course someone in the vicinity is making a kung fu movie), chicknaps a caterwauling twat, punches the tops off several buildings, and manages to sneak up on a surprising number of people seeing as he is, you know, a colossal, rampaging ape. The military, meanwhile, has other concerns ("The hell with the press. I'm gonna smoke this goddamned cigarette."), but eventually they step up and pummel A*P*E with artillery until he vomits blood. "Let's see him dance for his organ grinder now!" says one guy. Because his internal organs have just been grinded, I guess? That's pretty cold, dude.

The Ape Man

(1943)

Directed by William Beaudine

Why are people so impressed with Bela Lugosi? His turn as Dracula is laughably stagy and heavy-handed, and the rest of his resumé is just embarrassing, riddled with roles in shit like *Plan 9 from Outer Space* (widely considered by know-nothing bad-movie tourists to be the worst movie ever made), *Zombies on Broadway*, and *Bela Lugosi Meets a Brooklyn Gorilla*, the latter of which I probably should have included in this book but Bela had a pretty tragic life so I'll leave the poor man with *some* dignity. This flick fits in well with his oeuvre: the sound is so fucking bad that you can barely understand what people are saying, and the plot is so creaky and ridiculous that we're probably better off.

So, it turns out that this missing scientist isn't really missing after all; he's in hiding after accidentally turning himself into... Abraham Lincoln? Middle-aged Teen Wolf? Oh, wait, he's supposed to be an ape man, I guess. At least that dovetails with the title. The only cure: human spinal fluid. The caveat: the spinal fluid must be fresh. Optional: it should be extracted from a hot chick, while she's in her underwear. He sends his trained gorilla/life partner to obtain unwilling donors, while being opposed/irritated by a reporter who specializes in puff pieces, a spunky lady photographer, and a peeping tom. Highlights include someone referring to a photographer's camera as his "one-eyed monster", endless sexist comments regarding the lady photographer's overall competence (which turn out to be entirely justified), and the hilarious scene where ape man Bela's "cure" wears off and he can't stand upright anymore. Because apes are always all hunched over, see? Watching this goofy hack pretend to try to stand upright and fail (on both counts) might be one of the saddest/funniest things ever captured on film. And yes, that includes your cousin's wedding.

Attack of the Sabretooth

(2005)

Directed by George Miller

I'll be honest here, I think prehistoric mammals are way cooler than dinosaurs. Maybe it's just biological class loyalty, but give me dire wolves, Glyptodons, and giant sloths over Velociraptors any day. The absolute pimp of the dino-mammal world, of course, is the saber-toothed tiger, even if his oh-so-impressive teeth really are more practical for opening beers than for killing prehistoric super deer or whatever. The point is, I get that when the guy in this movie decided to develop a K-Mart version of Jurassic Park, saber-toothed tigers were at the very top of his list. Too bad it all goes south when these retarded college students show up and turn off his security system, allowing the saber-toothed tigers to escape. Okay, premise firmly established, all the moviemakers needed now were a big saber-toothed tiger puppet, a few hundred gallons of fake blood, and some chicks who were willing to take their shirts off and we'd have ourselves, at the very least, an A-/B+ outing here. I guess being on the verge of runaway success broke their brains though, because they decided to anti-wow us with *handicapped, bulimic saber-toothed tigers*. I swear to fucking God I'm not kidding. One of the saber-tooths (saber-teeth?) is completely paralyzed from the dick down, so it has to crawl pathetically after its intended victims, dragging its useless rear legs behind. (The scientists running the place should've built one of those "dog wheelchairs" for it. Can you imagine a saber-toothed tiger chasing people around while strapped into one of those contraptions? That would've been hilarious.) The only positives are the ~~tasteless~~ gruesome bit where a chick's guts are eaten while she watches, and the hot goth chick with the big nose who somehow manages *not* to be eaten. But if she's interested, I'll gladly volunteer for the job.

At the Earth's Core

(1976)

Directed by Kevin Connor

In the 1970s, a British studio called Amicus Productions decided to make three movies based on the works of Edgar Rice Burroughs, and correctly surmised that the Edgar Rice Burroughs stories people would most like to see would be the ones featuring dinosaurs. Well, it just so happened that E. Rice B (his rap name) had written a complete trilogy of dinosaur-centric novels: *The Land That Time Forgot*, *The People That Time Forgot*, and *Out of Time's Abyss*. So Amicus, showing the kind of foresight that ran them out of business a few months later, dutifully produced *The Land That Time Forgot* (1975), *The People That Time Forgot* (1977), and this garbage heap, which bears no relation to the other two and fuck you if you wanted to see the entire "That Time Forgot" trilogy filmed anyway.

So, Professor Grand Moff Tarkin and his "worst student" (his words) plan on driving their new invention, a gigantic drill, right through a mountain. Because that's just what the locals need, a perfectly good mountain with a hole in it. Unfortunately, they Amicus the whole thing up and end up at the center of the Earth's core, which is overflowing with Ugnaughts, goofy-ass monsters that would embarrass the Power Rangers, and cavemen who speak English. They take it all in stride until the younger guy finds out that the Ugnaughts are feeding all this hot snatch to some goony flying whatsits, at which point his dick takes over and he decides that it's time for *¡revolución!*. The story's full of stupid, oh-so-convenient horseshit (like the 4½-foot-long eyeglass cord), there's no tits, and G. M. Tarkin is constantly making bizarre statements that make no sense whatsoever or are just downright disturbing ("I have a firm grip upon your trousers, David!"). It's an inescapable pit of despair in movie form, and I will never, ever forgive Amicus for producing this instead of *Out of Time's Abyss*. Stupid limey assholes.

Aztec Rex

(2007)

Directed by Brian Trenchard-Smith

Jesus heart-ripping Christ, who knew ancient Aztec bitches were so fucking hot? Too bad a cartoon T. rex keeps eating all of them. Funny how when they teach you about the Aztecs in history class they never even mention the dinosaurs that wiped out their entire culture by gobbling up every decent piece of ass in sight. I guess it's "politically incorrect" to imply that if there were nothing left but fat chicks our current civilization would probably die out in a few generations too. Anyway, this is your typical, crappy Sci-Fi/Syfy/Syphilis Channel movie featuring a gigantic cartoon monster killing everybody, but I'm not surprised that it got the green light because not only does the elevator pitch rhyme ("Conquistadors versus dinosaurs!") but they managed to cast a main chick who truly is one of the pillars of fine, although she did go on to star in Joss Whedon's *Dollhouse* and I find it difficult not to hold that against her. Nevertheless, every time she's onscreen it's like the scent of orange blossoms blowing across the surface of a crystal-clear Mediterranean sea, the scene where she's repeatedly stabbing some guy in the stomach notwithstanding. I really wanted to end this review with an original poem celebrating her inimitable Aztec beauty, but I couldn't think of anything that rhymes with "Quetzalcoatl".

Baby: Secret of the Lost Legend

(1985)

Directed by B.W.L. Norton

If you think Pluto has had it rough, being downgraded to a lousy dwarf planet, imagine the emotional roller coaster Brontosaurus has been on. For decades he was one of the classics; a standard, really. Then, suddenly, Science decides that he didn't even exist! Old movies had to be re-edited, all known copies of *I Can Read About Dinosaurs!* were seized and burned, millions of little plastic toys (all of them inexplicably facing backwards) were recalled... And just as we were finally adjusting to a Brontosaurus-less world, Science did an about-face and decided that he really did exist after all. It's a good thing he's extinct, because believe me, this would have killed him. I know it's killing me; my whole angle for this review was going to be "HA HA BRONTOSAURUS DIDN'T EVEN EXIST YOU STUPID MOVIE LOLZ FAGS".

It starts at the African Child Endangerment Parade, where this guy is murdered and the pictures he's carrying – pictures of real, live dinosaurs – are stolen. Cut to our main chick, who's lost her enthusiasm for paleontology. "Some days you eat the bone, other days the bone eats you," says her husband.

I assume that's their code for "Why don't you take a break and give me a blowjob?" Wouldn't you know it though, these two boobs are the ones who all but trip over the dinosaurs in those pictures: three Brontosauruseses – two adults and a baby – that have somehow survived multiple mass extinctions and are just cool-cold-chilling it deep in the jungles of Africa. It's a mind-boggling moment that demands the epic, *sensawonder* treatment of a classic Steven Spielberg movie or the first time you got to third base, but this flick handles it like the grand opening of a new Steak 'n Shake when there's already an established Steak 'n Shake less than a mile away. I was more excited the last time they brought back the McRib, and I don't even like the McRib.

From here, *Baby: Secretion of the Lost Legend* is just another *E.T.* (1982) ripoff. There were tons of them at the time (*Short Circuit, Mac and Me, Harry and the Hendersons*), and *Baby* is hardly the worst of the odious, puke-inducing lot, but that's probably the best you can say about it. The bad guys needlessly kill one of the dinosaurs, clearly a beyond-endangered species that would be worth shit-tons more alive, and then just leave it there to rot in the jungle. Christ, at least use its feet to make novelty wastepaper baskets or something. The baby Brontosaurus, meanwhile, is spirited off by the good guys and dubbed "Baby", the most unimaginative name they could've possibly come up with. They should've named it "Emily". There is some family-friendly violence, and a lot of tits, but the former is flat and uninvolving , and the tits are all of the *National Geographic* variety, and I'm sorry but no one wants to see that because seriously, gross. Ultimately though, this is primarily a movie about a repulsively cute baby dinosaur getting underwear stuck on its head, accidentally kicking people in the nuts, and knocking shit over. One wonders why Hollywood ever felt the need to make a Marmaduke movie when they could've just re-released this.

Back to the Planet of the Apes

(1981)

Directed by Don Weis and Arnold Lavin

Okay, this one requires some setup, so here goes. Originally, there were five *Planet of the Apes* movies, followed by a TV series, and then a Saturday morning cartoon. The TV series bombed though, so they haphazardly cobbled various episodes together to make *five more* goddamned movies – with hilarious titles like *Life, Liberty, and Pursuit on the Planet of the Apes* – for a grand total of TEN *Planet of the Apes* movies, this one being #6 in the overall series. I suppose I could list all of them in order for your enlightenment, but fuck it, that's exactly the sort of thing the Internet is for.

So, after a cheesy intro by one of the main apes (which serves to set up the backstory while, they hope, justifying the existence of this horse-flogging nonsense), we meet our heroes, two astronauts who have gone through a time warp and crash-landed on the the Planet of the Apes. Now, I feel compelled to remind you that this is at least the *third* set of astronauts this has happened to. I'm not sure where all of these astronauts are coming from, but wherever it is you'd think someone back there would start looking into the matter. Anyway, these two kind of reminded me of Coy and

Vance, and if you remember who they are you probably also know the name of Boss Hogg's brother, which proves that you watched too much television as a kid and explains why you never get laid. (It's "Abraham Lincoln Hogg". And fuck you.) The apes chase Coy and Vance around for a while, until one of them (Coy? Vance? Who knows?) ends up trapped in an old subway tunnel alongside an ape and the two sides are forced to work together in order to save them, learning a valuable lesson in the process which they'll have forgotten entirely by the time the next aptly-named entry (*Forgotten City of the Planet of the Apes*) takes place. I make fun, but in all fairness this piecemeal, refuse-to-die pseudo-movie really isn't that bad for something that would probably have a hard time justifying its own existence in a court of law. Hell, compared to the 2001 remake it's practically a home run.

The Beast of Hollow Mountain

(1956)

Directed by Edward Nassour and Ismael Rodriguez

Two cowboys want to grow their cows in the same place, so naturally a range war erupts, which is kind of like a flame war except with more gunplay and less accusations of homosexuality. Actually, as range wars go this one is pretty mild; the worst that comes of it is a two-man brawl over an ugly chick. Still, these two clowns do manage to demolish an entire Mexican market in the process, and it's hard not to feel sorry for the affected Mexicans. They'll already poor as hell, barely scraping by by selling goods back and forth to one another in a completely unsustainable non-economy, and then these ten-gallon asshats show up and unapologetically wreck all their stuff while trying prove whose cock is bigger. Sure, all that crappy Mexican merchandise was probably only worth a grand total of two or three dollars in real money, but still. Later some cows disappear and the main cowboy reckons they've done been rustled, so he rounds up a few other cats to go look for them. Along the way, they pass by an old house, prompting this brilliant exchange:

"Who lives in that house?"

"Nobody - it's the abandoned house."

Classic. Anyway, in the end it turns out the guy rustling all the cows isn't a guy at all, it's a dinosaur. Now, "cowboys vs. dinosaurs" is obviously a marketable premise (witnessed by the fact that there are at least three movies sporting this very premise), but this flick could really use a few more dinosaurs and, frankly, more cowboys too. Then the lot of them could have engaged in an enormous donnybrook, possibly destroying an entire cowboy town in the process. That would've been epic, or at least hilarious. Instead, the big money scene is the dinosaur stampeding all the cows, which should come as no surprise given the unwritten movie rule that any time a cowboy movie introduces actual cows there has to be a scene where they stampede. Everyone always loses their shit when this happens, but I have yet to see a movie where anything bad ever comes of it – like the cows trampling a church picnic to death, or charging en masse over a cliff – so who cares? Let 'em stampede. Stupid cows.

The Beast that Killed Women

(1965)

Directed by Barry Mahon

"The Beast that Killed Women"

"Starring: Nudists"

There's something to be said for truth in advertising, but subtlety has its place too, you know? Anyway, the beast in question is a gorilla, and the action takes place at a nudist colony. Pre-production is now complete. Filming starts tomorrow.

So, after we're subjected to a parade of unwelcome casual nudity (it's mostly sub-sub-par women, all walking past the same tree) a gorilla shows up, for no reason, and kills this broad in an entirely G-rated fashion. Now, before we go on, I really want to emphasize this: a *gorilla* shows up at the *nudist colony* for *no reason*. That's the entire premise of this movie. At first everyone assumes that a homicidal sex maniac is on the loose, until the very next night when the gorilla is spotted hurling a guy into the lake. The best part? Nobody seems surprised by any of this. The cops just shrug their shoulders, set up an ambush, and shoot the gorilla the next time it shows itself. Case closed. Well, not quite - afterwards a well-to-do elderly woman is arrested, because apparently she was the owner of the escaped gorilla. Which, frankly, raises way more questions than it answers. Also, what the hell is going on in her neighborhood when the detectives arrive to take her in? It sounds like there's a huge brawl going on just off camera involving several small children and a flock of ducks. Jesus Christ, why aren't they calling that in?

In this day of Rule 34 some may find this movie charming in its idiotic, trashy innocence, but I'm not here to be charmed I'm here to be entertained, and that's not likely to happen when a movie's sole selling point is "naked, ugly women". The only time I find naked, ugly women entertaining is when I'm half-blind drunk, and then only if they're crying or falling down the stairs.

Beneath the Planet of the Apes

(1970)

Directed by Ted Post

The best thing about this first sequel to *The Planet of the Apes* (1968) is how it gleefully opens up a whole new can of "What the fuck?" The original movie contains two shocking twists; one of these, obviously, is given away by the title, and the other one is given away on the cover of at least some DVD editions (thanks, assholes). But Part 2 here is crammed with so much insanity that you have to watch it twice just to catch it all. More astronauts inexplicably crash-land on the Planet of the Apes. (By the sixth movie this would go from "unfathomable, odds-defying coincidence" to "a typical Tuesday". Seriously, some enterprising apes should've tracked down the exit point of that time warp and opened up a combination information booth/concession stand.) The main guy from the first movie is chased around the desert by illusions, and eventually vanishes into thin air. (By all accounts, exactly what the actor playing this cat wanted to do in real life when it came to these *Planet of the Apes* movies.) There's a fight on a runaway stagecoach, a tiresome western trope so out of place here you might not even notice that it's part of an extended, go-nowhere series of events included in the narrative solely to kill time. We learn that there are ape hippies. The main guy drinks standing water that clearly has dirt and God knows what floating in it, and is surprised when it tastes bad. The apes go to war against a bunch of burn ward refugees who have ESP and worship a super A-bomb stolen from the Alpha Omega house. The main guy takes great pride in openly defying the ESP coalition, even though, logically, they should be his allies. ESP is used to pull a "Plato's Stepchildren" and make the two main guys fight. (This is one of the most homoerotic fights in film history, by the way.) And at the end the super A-bomb detonates and destroys the entire planet, which you'd think would preclude them from making of any more sequels, but it didn't.

Definitely my favorite *Planet of the Apes* movie, if only for the sheer blathering insanity of it all.

Fun Fact: The shot of post-nuke New York in this movie was re-purposed as a shot of post-nuke San Francisco for an episode of the classic TV series *Sledge Hammer!* You won't learn shit like that reading one of Leonard Maltin's crummy books.

The Black Scorpion

(1957)

Directed by Edward Ludwig

Apparently when the two cowpokes (heh) in *The Beast of Hollow Mountain* trashed that Mexican market it was just the latest in a long line of hardships visited upon our hardworking neighbors to/from the south. Because according to this movie, volcanos have been making the lives of Mexico's peasants hell for centuries. (Seriously, scriptwriter, have you ever even been to Mexico? They do have cities too, you know.) And things are about to get a lot worse, because when you're a peasant, they always do. Giant, prehistoric scorpions, large enough to derail a train, have been freed from the impacted bowels of the earth and are on the rampage. "I beg of you all not to lose your heads. In any sense of the word," recommends one expert. He's a comedian. Despite their goofy, distinctly non-scorpion-like eyes (Stop looking at me!), and the fact that, in some shots, they're entirely transparent, the giant scorpions are pretty damned cool, and they kill a considerable number of people, which is the only real way to gauge a giant scorpion's worth. Our hero, meanwhile, cracks racist jokes and, at one point, indicates a baby in a cradle by casually pointing a loaded revolver at it. And he's not even the most odious character in this movie: that honor belongs to this annoying Mexican child who must be practicing to sneak over the border because he's constantly stowing away inside crane cages and under tarps only to reveal himself at the worst possible moment. Every time someone opened a goddamned bottle of aspirin I expected his spic ass to come rolling out and start rattling off apologies and compliments. He's simultaneously a total liability, a racist stereotype, and a shameless ass-kisser. Dying is too good for the likes of him, which means that, naturally, he survives. So yeah, it's a movie rife with hopeless idiots, but the monsters are cool and, overall, I liked it. I was actually surprised to learn that this perfectly respectable movie was once mocked on *Mystery Science Theater 3000*. I guess you can make fun of anything if you're cynical enough.

BloodMonkey

(2007)

Directed by Robert Young

That funky monkey. Seriously though, if you've committed yourself to calling your movie "BloodMonkey" you really need to concentrate on two things: 1) learning where the space key is on your laptop and 2) delivering on the blood. This movie fails on both counts. Several dullards are exploring this mysterious, isolated valley, led by a sketchy professor and his unbelievable cunt of an assistant. (The assistant really is a clit beyond compare. I would trade a year of my life for ten minutes alone with her, a baseball ball, a straight razor, and a box of salt. Oh, and some condoms.) (Hey, I didn't say she was ugly.) It's painfully obvious that the professor is up to no good, but everyone blindly follows him anyway and a long, *long* eventually later they pay for their gullibility when they're pissed on by giant monkeys. You read that right - *pissed on*. Hey, if that's your bag, makers of *BloodMonkey*, I'm not here to judge, but trust me when I tell you that the rest of us would really rather not know about it.

Bride of the Gorilla

(1951)

Directed by Curt Siodmak

If you've ever heard Orson Welles pretend to be humble or flip out over frozen peas you know what a self-important SOB he was, so I'll bet he loved it when people reminded him that he once appeared in this piece of crap. He probably tried to suck off every... Oops, wait a minute, that's not Orson Welles, it's Perry Mason. Well, whatever; they're basically the same guy.

It seems that everyone in the jungle wants to fuck the boss's wife: "She looks good to any man. That's a compliment to you," someone tells her husband. ("Thanks. I fell in love with her the moment I realized I was so awesome.") Perry Mason earns the honor after he makes her a widow by pushing her husband down in the general vicinity of a non-venomous snake, subsequently becoming husband #2 in record fucking time. Seriously, I don't think #1 had even reached room temperature yet. The local witch decides to balance the books, so she doses Perry with a mysterious drug that makes him think he's sporadically turning into a gorilla. This leads to several questions, the most important one being: *Where do I get the shit this old bat has access to?* Seriously, the drugs in bad movies are always so much better than the drugs in real life could ever hope to be. Somebody needs to sequester themselves in a lab and perfect this gorilla stuff, pronto. Can you imagine that shit kicking in right in the middle of a job interview? Or during a traffic stop? Man, your life would never be boring again. And best of all, I'm relatively certain that it's impossible to successfully prosecute a gorilla. Of course there's probably a better-than-average chance that you'd end up riddled with bullets and falling to your death from the Ferris wheel you just scaled after your carnival-trashing rampage, but hey, that's the price you pay, junkie.

Carnival Magic

(1981)

Directed by Al Adamson

There's nothing like a chintzy, old-school traveling carnival. The rip-off attractions, the poorly-maintained rides, the bargain-basement dancing girls... The world is a sadder place now that stricter safety codes and increased enforcement of solicitation laws have put so many of them out of business. The carnival in this movie has fallen on hard times like all the rest, but then the boss's daughter learns that their resident magician owns an honest-to-fuck talking monkey! So how do they take advantage of this? They develop a stage show where the monkey stands around making stupid comments while the magician and his ~~lovely~~ assistant perform their horrible, also-ran magic act. Are you fucking kidding me??? Dude, it's a goddamned TALKING MONKEY and that's the best you can come up with? Hell, just sit that fucker on a wooden crate and let him read from the collected works of Shakespeare or Tucker Max and you'd be doing a far better job of exploiting his talents. Not that I'd actually want to see this in practice, because the producers didn't try all that hard to make it look like the monkey is actually talking. Sometimes its lips move, sometimes they don't, and in both cases the overall effect is indescribably off-putting and disturbing. I'm glad I wasn't on hallucinogens while I was watching this flick. For real, it has "bad trip" written all over it.

Naturally the talking monkey soon gets up to some monkey**shines**, like when it steals a station wagon – accidentally kidnapping a fat chick in the process – and gets into a car chase with the cops. (*Of course* banjo music plays during this part.) The monkey doesn't go to jail though, and frankly nobody seems all that impressed with any of its worldview-altering antics, aside from one scientist who wants to study it to see if it's the missing link. Everyone else is too busy having G-rated romance, philosophizing, or just sort of hanging around. Eventually someone kidnaps the monkey and sells it to the scientist, who has some pretty specific plans for the little bastard: "*Vivisection* is a dirty word, but it is necessarily for it to solve problems that must be solved," he says. Awesome. Also, what?

Seriously, I don't even know where to begin. Everything about this movie is disturbing beyond words, from the slipshod talking monkey, to the guy who wants his daughter to dress like a boy and answer to "Bud", to the magician who may or may not have animal ESP, to the midget who shows up out of nowhere to deliver one line ("Hi, Sheriff!"), to the savage, drunken beat-down the bad guy gives his girlfriend, to the carny raid on the scientist's private care center, to the part where the monkey tries to *commit suicide,* right up to the very, very end where they promise a Part 2. It's an endless nightmare of insanity.

Carnosaur

(1993)

Directed by Adam Simon

Carnosaur is the *Piranha* to *Jurassic Park's Jaws*, but while *Piranha* is an excellent movie in its own right, *Carnosaur* is such a muddled disaster that fifteen minutes in I still had no idea what was going on. We've got a baby dinosaur escaping from a poultry farm, a drunk waving a gun around, a hot blonde sabotaging construction equipment, and endless ominous notations about how many infected cells per million everyone has, as if this is somehow generating suspense when we have no idea what the hell they're even talking about.

The baby dinosaur soon chews up several nobs, while a fully-grown specimen that appears to be housed in a discotheque is used to take out a witness who didn't actually witness anything. "Oh, what the hell is going on?" asks the drunk at this point, echoing my thoughts exactly. There's some gore, hippies are dismembered, dinosaurs hatch out of chicken eggs that were earmarked for public consumption (just like the anti-GMO people have been warning us), Richie "Opie" Cunningham's mongoloid brother is decapitated, women inexplicably pop baby dinosaurs out of their twats, and the bitch responsible for it all is allowed to prattle on for far too long by someone who has the opportunity to put us all out of our misery by simply shooting her. For real, I can't even recall the last time I saw such a simple premise ("dinosaur eats people") convoluted up to such a ridiculous degree. Borderline nonsensical and utterly hopeless, so naturally there were two sequels.

Carnosaur II

(1995)

Directed by Louis Morneau

Carnosaur 1 was such a financial success that not only did I lose all faith in humanity, but they made (to date) two sequels. Now, I'm not gonna pretend to understand what's going on in these miserable movies, but this one kicks off with invisible(?) dinosaurs raiding the mess hall at an isolated scientific facility. Shortly thereafter, some jokers who have been called in to fix the wiring or something (priorities, right?) show up, wander around for a while, and are attacked by carnosaurs. One carnosaur bitch-slaps the token black guy (twice!) before eating him; another carnosaur somehow manages to conceal itself in the back of a helicopter and take out the sole hottie when she boards, never mind the fact that there are very few places inside a helicopter where a midget could hide, much less a goddamned dinosaur; and the dumb climax involves a kid risking everyone's life to go back and fight the boss dinosaur when the entire facility is counting down to explode so obviously the prehistoric bastard is going to die regardless. Pretty terrible, but in all honestly I kinda liked it anyway. It's gory, and at least the simplified, streamlined story made some kind of sense, making it, if nothing else, marginally better than Part 1. "Marginally better than *Carnosaur 1*." There's a quote for the movie poster.

Carnosaur 3: Primal Species

(1996)

Directed by Jonathan Winfrey

Terrorists think they're jacking a load of uranium, but nope, it's carnosaurs. The authorities are quickly on the scene, but they're pretty much in the dark, convinced that they're dealing with "Arab smack peddlers" or "Eurotrash" looking to build a nuclear bomb. (To detonate at the the big rave in Amsterdam, I guess?) When the truth finally ~~smacks them in the~~ eats their face a commando unit is sent in with orders to take the carnosaurs alive, so they pump round after round of ammo into the dinosaurs, apparently unclear on the concepts of "alive" or "orders". *Carnosaur 3*, meanwhile, is unclear on the concept of "not sucking". It takes place almost entirely in a single warehouse (at least until they corner the dinos on a cargo ship and it turns into a carnosaur *Under Siege*); it's chintzier than Parts 1 & 2 put together (a shot of the cargo ship pulling out to sea, for example, appears to be stock footage of a ship being pushed *into* port by tugboats, run backwards); and there's entirely too much tough-guy posturing, a problem with movies featuring military commandos since at least *Predator* (1987). And don't say "Well at least *Predator* got it right!" because *Predator* is highly overrated and I should know because I'm a professional movie critic and you're not.

So yeah, *Carnosaur 3* jobs it. But what else did you expect from an action movie starring "Nick" from *Family Ties*? "Yo, Mallory!" Duh.

Caved In: Prehistoric Terror

(2006)

Directed by Richard Pepin

The frog mafia wants to claim some emeralds located in an old salt mine, so instead of simply sneaking in there and taking them they contrive this moronic, convoluted scheme that involves multiple potential witnesses and therefore necessitates killing everyone in sight. Complicating things further are 1) a cave-in and 2) giant, prehistoric beetles that show up and start killing everybody. As luck would have it though the mob guys just happen to be armed with laser rifles that...

Okay, you know what? Fuck off. *There's no such thing as consumer-grade laser rifles, you stupid fucking movie.* If this story were set in the future, fine, but it's not. Christ, you're already trying to sell us on a criminal plot that makes zero sense perpetrated by French people who don't immediately surrender at the first sign of trouble. Stop treating us like imbeciles. The only decent scene in this entire movie is when one of the bugs explodes and its thick, creamy guts spooge all over this fluffy teenage girl's face and hair. And she'd better get used to it, because with *Caved In: Prehistoric Terror* on her resumé there's probably going to be a very similar scene in every movie she's cast in from now on.

Cavegirl

(1985)

Directed by David Oliver

I'm an acknowledged expert on obscure pop culture of the 1980s (it was the easiest major my college offered), but even I had completely forgotten that this movie existed until I started doing research for this book. Which is funny because it really is the quintessential '80s comedy. It's got a dumb, almost desperate premise, a put-upon nerd as the hero, lots of tits, and features synth-pop music by bands so obscure that the only one who's ever heard of them is that creepy old guy who always shows up for '80s night and hits on girls half his age. He usually manages to take one home too, because he says he has a yacht. He doesn't though. He's a serial killer.

Anyway, our main guy, the nerd, lucks out while on a field trip, because thanks to a criminally irresponsible scientific experiment (conducted without notice, on someone else's property) he's sent back in time to the dawn of man, where he has at least *some* chance of getting laid. And wouldn't you know it, the first cavegirl he meets is cute, blonde, has perfect teeth, shaves her legs, and from all indications is lice-free. (In a nod to realism though, the nerd does insist that she put on some deodorant before he sexually molests her.) And there are a few other cave people hanging around too. They fall down a lot. Hollywood screenwriters have assured me that this is hilarious.

Now might be a good time to make a sandwich or talk to your needy girlfriend, because almost nothing happens during the second act. Oh, there's farting, of course, and an endless bit where the main guy is pursued by an annoying fat chick. (Dude, it's caveman times - no one will call you out if you just punch her in the face.) Mostly everyone just sits around waiting for the movie to end. It's very relatable. Finally, though, there is a crisis: I really had to shit. It was a nasty one, too - Wendy's. And by the time I got back, something was actually happening: the Falling Down People had been captured by bigger, stronger, cannibal-er cave people. Using modern prank technology, the nerd manages to scare the cannibals away, and, having saved the day, he's now free to knock ~~boots~~ bare feet with his (cave) girl, who likely-as-not has some sort of incurable Stone Age VD but hey, nerds in the 1980s had to take what they could get. It wasn't like today, when even the hottest girls enjoy *The Big Bang Theory* and want a guy who knows how to wipe the virus off their laptop after they click on the wrong cat video.

So yeah, *Cavegirl* is pretty wretched, but it does feature some kickass songs by the band SSQ. And yes, I recognized them immediately; I have their debut album on vinyl. Did you know that their lead singer went on to become Stacy Q, who recorded the song "Two of Hearts"? You're right, I *do* know a lot about '80s music. I'm surprised a girl your age is so into it. I agree, age *ain't* nothin' but a number! You are a very cool and perceptive young lady!

Would you like to see my yacht?

Caveman

(1981)

Directed by Carl Gottlieb

The Beatles were known for making pointless, plotless movies where they just ran around being talentless and stupid, but this flick was that approach taken to its most absurd extreme, at least until *Give My Regards to Broad Street* came out.

Ringo Starr, everyone's least favorite Beatle (it's on his resumé), plays a caveman who is endlessly hassled by killer plants, other cavemen, and dinosaurs that would look *really* cool if they weren't intentionally designed to look silly and fake, thus violating the first rule of movie comedy, i.e. a comedy shouldn't act like it knows it's funny. Of course, this shitty movie isn't funny, which just proves my point. Or... refutes it? I'm... I'm actually a little confused right now. Let's move on.

Since this movie takes place before the existence of language (or quality) there's isn't any dialogue at all, just grunting, followed by embarrassment for everyone involved, and utter dissatisfaction when it's all over. It's the cinematic equivalent of a hate fuck. "Hilarious" gags include Ringo Starr getting high, "funny" sound effects, farting, people falling down, a blind man bumping into things, feces, attempted rape, and a guy with a leg injury hopping around on one foot because this is a joke, apparently. Oh, and there's a giant egg, because that's funny, I guess. An egg. But, like, it's a really BIG egg. Comedy gold, if you're a talentless hack whose mother is a whore. To be fair, one bit does *almost* work: the meta joke where the cavemen discover music. See, because prehistoric music is the only music older and more irrelevant than the Beatles.

On the plus side, a pretty cool pterodactyl shows up for one scene, and Shelley "Diane from *Cheers*" Long (playing, I dunno, Cavegirl #3, I guess) looks uncommonly good here, trumped only by her turn in panties and knee-high socks in 1982's *Night Shift*. Not only would I fuck Shelley Long as she appears in this movie, but I might actually like it.

Cavemen (Unaired Pilot)

(2007)

Written by Joe Lawson

Back in 2006-2007 the guy who created the funniest TV show of all time, *Sledge Hammer!*, and one of the cats who made *Police Squad!* (like the fifth funniest TV show of all time) teamed up to make a new show called *Crime Squad!* for ABC. It would ruthlessly mock the endless *CSI* spin-offs and clones then stinking up the airwaves, and they even hoped to include Frank Drebin (the main detective from *Police Squad!*) and Sledge Hammer (the main detective from... you figure it out) as minor characters who would show up from time to time. It's inarguably the greatest television program that ever could have happened, and it almost did, but ABC changed their minds and went with this show instead, which if you're reading this in the future is based on a series of television commercials for *car insurance*. Given people's general distaste for car insurance (a mandatory non-product that basically amounts to gambling, at sucker odds, against an opponent who won't pay up if you win), *Cavemen* was probably doomed from the start, but ABC really wasn't prepared for how much test audiences hated the first episode (which they were too scared to even air) or how hard the retooled version ultimately tanked. Of course this is exactly what they deserved, and I hope lots of people got fired, went into a downward life spiral, and ultimately took their own lives over it. But was the show really that bad? Let's watch that unaired pilot and find out.

So, the big joke is that you buy the company's insurance, but then when you got into an accident or whatever they deny your claim and you end up with nothing, even though you've paid them thousands of dollars in premiums over the years, because they have lobbyists in Washington and you don't so ha ha, fuck you. Oops, sorry, wrong joke. The big joke *in the commercials* was that the cavemen were intelligent and articulate, but people still treated them like, well, cavemen. It's a passable gag for a thirty-second commercial, and way better than plenty of other TV commercials from the time, like that smug, repulsive, uncanny-valley talking baby in the E*Trade spots that any sane parent would have left in a hot car for as long as it took. Fuck you, E*Trade baby. You should've been the ad for the morning-after pill.

Anyway, despite what some people think, what works in a thirty-second TV spot can easily work as a thirty-minute TV show. You just have to do the same thing 59 more times. The problem arose when they encouraged the test audience to really think about what they were watching and *oh my god the cavemen are stand-ins for black people*. The slur for cavemen is "magger" (from Cro-Magnon). There's a scene where the cavemen criticize an obvious caveman stand-in for Al Roker ("Dance for the Man, monkey."). And the main plot point of this episode? One of the cavemen is dating a white girl and her father doesn't approve! Seriously, this shit is so subversive I can't believe it actually exists, and it's no wonder people got all riled up about it because it's kind of fucking brilliant. Oh, and while it's probably not *Crime Team!* funny, it is pretty damn funny. I've never seen the "retooled" version that did air (and flopped), but there's no need to; *this* is what they should've gone with. Shame on you, ABC. Your pussies can probably be seen from space.

The Clan of the Cave Bear

(1986)

Directed by Michael Chapman

Not being a bored housewife who gave up on my dreams years ago, I never read any of the *Clan of the Cave Bear* novels (there were several), but my understanding is that they're essentially caveman smut. Caveman porn: proof that Rule 34 existed long before the Internet. This movie version, meanwhile, ostensibly exists solely as an excuse for the mermaid from *Splash* (1984) to finally show us her tits, but she stubbornly conceals the goods like they're made of magic fairy gold so I guess *that* was a wash. Whatever, prude. They're probably lopsided anyway. As you'd expect, the story itself is pretty slight: the main chick is a cavegirl who's separated from her tribe then adopted by a rival tribe from another hood where she's endlessly victimized by this cave dude who doesn't know that no means no and rape is rape. Later she's (briefly) banished from this tribe for being a liberated woman, pops out a kid, and eventually decides to pursue a career in pharmacy. It's a terrible movie, but it's funnier than *Caveman* (1981), the main chick looks pretty tasty as a teenager (when she's played by Nicole Eggert, AKA the hot-ass daughter from *Charles in Charge*), and at one point there is a fight with an actual cave bear. It tears one caveguy's head clean off! Take that, whitey.

I watched this one with my dad, and when it was over he nodded sagely and said "Yup. That's really how it was back then." Like he was actually there or something.

Congo

(1995)

Directed by Frank Marshall

Jaws (1975) is to *The Deep* (1977) as *Jurassic Park* (1993) is to _______?

The correct answer is *Congo*. This is the only time that the correct answer will ever be *Congo*.

Diamond-hunters run afoul of killer apes, but never fear, the response team just happens to have access to a *talking gorilla* that can...

Arrgghh, god *dammit.* Writing that just made me dumber. I could actually feel part of my brain permanently shutting down. (If you don't think this movie sounds *that* preposterous, try this: imagine the exact same premise, but substitute a pack of wolves, and a talking dog.) Admittedly, *Congo* does wear its cheese badge openly on its sleeve, trotting out cornball actors like Bruce Campbell, the realtor from *Poltergeist*, Joe Don "Mitchell" Baker, Dr. Frank N. Furter, and the black Ghostbuster. It's like this flick is daring us to take it seriously. The cast sure doesn't, yukking it up or sleepwalking through their stupefyingly bad dialogue like they're doing this gig for free or something. "I don't have a price I'm not a pound of sugar I'm a primatologist!" (Note lack of punctuation/enunciation in this "actor's" delivery.)

Jesus Christ, how did the screenwriter's WGA card not burst into flames? Maybe the talking fucking monkey wrote the script. Speaking of, why why why, in what is purportedly an action movie, is the talking gorilla portrayed like the monkey in an detestable family comedy with a title like "Monkey Business" or "Monkeying Around" or "Funky Monkey"? (Seriously, fuck you, Hollywood.) It drinks martinis, insults women, belches, smokes... Monkeys less slapstick than this have won the Cannonball Run. Then we've got people carrying the gorilla around like it's a swooning debutante or something. Are you fucking kidding me? Do you know how heavy a goddamned gorilla is? None of this is as embarrassing as the ridiculous, goofy-ass hippo attack though. (Yes, I know hippos are incredibly dangerous in real life, but there's a reason "hippo attack" hasn't become a standard adventure movie trope.) And are they really so uninventive that they're going to end this movie with an erupting volcano? Of course they are. Still, the ~~thrilling~~ deranged climax, featuring the main chick blasting killer apes with a goddamned laser rifle, is so gloriously insane that one is tempted to forgive everything. Ditto the nighttime standoff with the apes, all drenched in fog and illuminated with purple night-vision lighting, blue motion-detecting lasers, and random flashes of gunfire. It's like the world's weirdest-themed disco.

Conquest of the Planet of the Apes

(1972)

Directed by J. Lee Thompson

By the time of this Planet of the Apes movie (#4) we've traveled back in time from the post-apocalypse original to 1991, an era where Vanilla Ice rules the airwaves, *Terminator 2: It's the Exact Same Movie, Idiots* dominates the box office, and dogs and cats are no more, wiped out by a mysterious, pet-targeting plague. There's even a memorial in their honor. The dog statue sitting on top of this memorial is identified as "Rover", but the cat statue doesn't seem to have a name. "Fuck it," the sculptor probably said, "he wouldn't come when you called him anyway." Regardless, since there aren't any more dogs or cats, people have adopted a new household pet: apes.

Okay, what? I mean fine, for the purposes of this movie is stupid I'll accept the premise that dogs and cats are extinct. But replacing them with *apes?* Not bunnies, or sugar gliders, or quokkas, but motherfucking *apes?* That's absurd. Not to mention the fact that the highly-trainable, man-like apes in question basically serve as slaves, making the entire premise super racist too. There's a hyper-intelligent ape from the future secretly in their midst though, and he has a dream (See?), so it's not long before he *vivas* the very *la revolución* that the humans have spent the entire movie wringing their hands over in anticipatory dread but have all but ensured with their jaw-droppingly moronic decisions. Stupid assholes. This wouldn't have happened if they'd gone with bunnies.

The Crater Lake Monster

(1977)

Directed by William R. Stromberg

Not to be confused with the "crater-*faced* monster", AKA my date to the senior prom. It started as a cruel bet: who could find the ugliest date for prom? Little did I know that by the end of the night I'd end up falling for my "joke" date. (As it turned out, she was pretty easy, and had amazing tits.) So a valuable lesson was learned by all, a vengeful ex-girlfriend pushed the guy who came up with the bet into the giant novelty prom cake, and it all ended with a Crowded House song. Er, hang on... maybe that was a movie I saw on cable. Does that plot sound familiar to anyone?

Anyway, the crater *lake* monster is a plesiosaur, riled up by a meteor strike, that takes to eating people, including one luckless drip who drives in from an entirely different movie after robbing a liquor store. This flick is more concerned with killing time than people though; it's full of endless, pointless scenes that go no place, the most unbearable of which feature these two bickering, co-dependent yokels. The dinosaur itself – a product of top-notch cheesy old-school effects – looks great, but what good is a dinosaur movie that's 10% meat and 90% filler? "Things always look hopeless when you're sober," says somebody at one point. You got that right, chief, if by "sober" you mean "waiting for the dinosaur scenes in *The Crater Lake Monster*" and by "hopeless" you mean "When are these two yokels going to admit to each other what the rest of us already know and just have gay sex already?" What a waste of time. Fuck this movie.

The Devil's Gift

(1984)

Directed by Kenneth J. Berton

This dotty old bat conjures up something horrible while playing with her Parker Brothers™ brand ouija (card)board, and it proceeds to burn her toy house to the ground before taking up residence in one of those cymbal-banging monkey dolls. Now, it's common knowledge that wind-up, cymbal-playing monkey dolls are evil – not to mention annoying – so why the main guy's special lady friend decides to later give the monkey in question to his son as a birthday present is a complete mystery. (On the plus side, he also gets the Star Wars Imperial AT-AT, the lucky bastard.) Soon our main guy is suffering from nightmares, including that one where you find yourself inexplicably naked in a public place, which isn't exactly a horror movie nightmare but this entire exercise is textbook unclear on the concept so I'm not really surprised that they messed this up. Via its evil powers of annoyance (or vice-versa, whatever) the toy monkey soon kills the houseplants, a fly, a goldfish, *and* the family dog. Then it possesses the main guy's lady friend and, using her, tries to murder his son. When the monkey is finally identified as the culprit Dad realizes that it has to go, but for some reason he feels he has to *trick* the toy into falling into a bag before he can simply discard it the curbside trash. Okay, acting is hard under any circumstances (not really), but pretending to put one over on an inanimate object is way beyond this particular actor's abilities and the end result is indescribably stupid and hilarious ("Bingo!"). Like the proverbial cat though (disclaimer: not actually a proverb) the monkey comes back, so Dad decides to get rid of it once and for all by burying it in a field. The monkey summons a goddamned EARTHQUAKE though and... oh my god, the sight of this guy (clearly a badly-made puppet) hanging over a ledge as the earth attempts to swallow him up is hysterical. Plus: the main guy bashing *The Bride of Frankenstein* (1935) for not being scary, (like *The Devil's Gift* is so much better, dick), and an appearance by that classic 1970s pickup line "Hey baby, what's happening?"

Blatantly stolen from an old Stephen King story, so see it before King seizes every known copy and then hires Mick Garris to make an even stupider version.

Dino Dan "Where the Dinosaurs Are"

(2010)

Written by J.J. Johnson and Christin Simms

Dino Dan is a children's program about a little boy who is so knowledgeable about dinosaurs that you'll want to punch him right in his know-it-all face. You know the type of kid I'm talking about: they pick some pet subject – usually dinosaurs or something to do with outer space – devour everything they can find out about it, and then constantly find reasons to bring it up in everyday conversation, going on and on and on until you can't take it anymore and actually end up punishing them for learning. This kid takes it ever further though. He's so into dinosaurs that he actually suffers from complex delusions, seeing them literally everywhere and even engaging in "adventures" in which "bad" dinosaurs commit crimes he's obviously committing himself. In this episode, for example, Dan and his friends (including a chick named Kami, who is certifiably TYTBSH) (that's Too Young To Be So Hot) are visiting a museum, where he decides to steal a valuable fossil he's unwisely been entrusted with. He subsequently blames the theft first on a Compsognathus, and later still on two other dinosaurs whose names I missed, although I believe one of them was a Styrachanachapollywallasaurus. (Note to any real-life Dans out there: do not write in to correct me on this, or I will become Facebook friends with your teenage sister and teach her several horrific new ways to torment you.) Tragically, Dan's friends are unapologetic enablers, so his delusions persist and when he ultimately decides to return the stolen fossil he perceives himself as the hero of the story, instead of the burgeoning sneak-thief he actually is. It's a disturbing portrait of mental illness, to be sure. The fact that there's an entire series based around this ass nugget is bad enough, but there's also a spin-off starring his little brother, who ALSO goes on and on about dinosaurs until you want to punt him into next Thursday. Talk about an irritating trend. Give me *Hannah Montana* or *iCarly* any day.

Dino-Riders "The Adventure Begins"

(1987)

Written by Carla and Gerry Conway

Some rack-and-pinion idiots from the future travel to the past where they fight dinosaurs and, eventually, fight each other *with* dinosaurs. It's a can't-miss idea, but only if you're eight years old, which, incidentally, is what someone should've told the producers of the TV series *Terra Nova* (2011). As for the Dino-Riders, their VHS tape reeks of something you'd get for free if you mailed away enough proofs of purchase, and it's so shameless that there's actually commercial breaks featuring ads for other toys from the makers of Dino-Riders. That might be forgivable though if this cartoon wasn't so miserably generic and at least *tried* to make sense. Here's an example: the good guys (a bunch of white bread pansies called – ugh – "Valorians") can communicate with the dinosaurs via ESP and immediately befriend several of them. So why, when a T. rex later attacks, do they ask the other dinosaurs for help instead of just ESPing the T. rex and telling him to cool it? As usual, the bad guys are far more interesting: their leader is a toad wearing a spacesuit, and his cronies include humanoid snakes and bipedal hammerhead sharks. See, this is why toy lines fail. What kid is gonna root for a bunch of generic pretty-boy douchebags over a *walking hammerhead shark?* Like most things people manage to fuck up anyway, it really is a no-brainer. As a result, the only Dino-Rider figures any kid ever asked for were the "evil" ones, leaving no one for them to fight. Which meant that the only "adventures" available for them to act out were "Dino Riders: Petty Infighting", "Dino-Riders: Early Retirement", and, much later of course, "Dino-Riders: Journey to eBay".

The Dinosaur Chronicles

(2004)

Directed by John Polonia and Mark Polonia

The Dinosaur Chronicles is actually two short movies, each stupider than the other. In the first short, three dweebs go back in time and end up stranded on an island full of dinosaur effects stolen from another movie. They're attacked by some puppets and the worst giant spider since *Nude for Satan* (1974), and one guy gets shit on by a pterodactyl. They don't starve though, because at one point they stumble upon a downed plane loaded with Tupperware containers full of breakfast cereal. (If you were one of the people who donated to USA for Africa in the 1980s, I hope you realize that this is what your money bought.) I guess the writer couldn't think of anything else to happen after that because suddenly a volcano erupts and our heroes only manage to survive by jumping into the swimming pool. The guy who's drunk literally the entire time is kind of funny – even while puking, he stops to take a drink – but other than that this is pretty awful.

In the second short World War Part 3 has finally occurred and you know who comes back after that. No, not Jesus - dinosaurs. Two dorks who are hiding from the dinosaurs in an office building decide they need to whack some drip named Caesar. ("What is this guy, a living salad?" says one.

Ha ha! You asshole.) First they look for Caesar in the basement; he isn't there, but one of the dorks gets killed by a dinosaur puppet. I don't know how he plans to pull it off since he's only packing a squirt gun, but the remaining dork is determined to complete their mission, so he tenaciously tracks Caesar down and barges in on him while he's playing video games. Then the movie just stops.

Suck my warm-blooded balls, *Dinosaur Chronicles*.

The Dinosaur Hunter

(2000)

Directed by Rick Stevenson

The back of the DVD case does everything short of driving to your house and lying to your face to give the impression that this is a movie about people hunting a real, live dinosaur, which is total bullshit because it's actually about people hunting for dinosaur *fossils*. Not since *Massacre in Dinosaur Valley* (1985) has a movie with "dinosaur" in the title been such a bait & switch hose job, but at least *Massacre in Dinosaur Valley* favored us with Susan Hahn's impeccable tits, plus gobs of outrageous violence. *The Dinosaur Hunter*, conversely, is a family film, aptly set in the Great Depression, and it begins when TV's Manimal, dressed in his finest Indiana Jones cosplay, arrives in this destitute Dust Bowl burg offering $500 (a small fortune in *Grapes of Wrath* era money) to anyone who can help him locate an intact dinosaur skeleton. Of course the local minister is entirely against this, Christians generally being against anything involving science, logic, or simple human decency. I mean, why earn some desperately-needed cash doing honest work when you can just come to church on Sunday and beg an elusive, mystical ghost for the money? Oh, and don't forget to tithe. There's also an evil paleontologist who dresses like a cartoon hobo and is probably a distant relative of the evil meteorologist from *Twister*, and a magical negro with ESP, a super-racist stereotype that would've barely been acceptable if this movie had been MADE in the 1930s. In the plus column, the town hottie looks like what would happen if Ellie Kemper and Jewel Staite somehow had a baby together, and she conspicuously moistens up every time Manimal so much as glances in her direction; there's a scene where the main kids' dad shoots the bad guy's wooden leg off; and this same bad guy is ultimately crushed to death beneath a gigantic dinosaur skull. Given this unexpected level of violence (a "low++" at best, but still more than I expected), not to mention Ellie & Jewel's love child dripping all over Manimal like a leaky faucet, when the dust cleared (heh) I had no choice but to declare this one a winner. Not bad for a family movie.

Dinosaur Island

(1994)

Directed by Fred Olen Ray and Jim Wynorski

Ah, to be thirteen years old again. Sure, it's almost impossible to get laid (except by a teacher) and you spend a lot of time getting beat up on the bus, but at least I'd be in a position to enjoy this movie, which can be entirely summed up in three words: "dinosaurs and boobies". After their plane goes down in the drink an "Army career man" (as opposed to a career Army man, I guess) and the prisoners he's escorting wash up on an uncharted island inhabited by cave women sporting fake tits (supplied by ancient aliens, no doubt), superimposed dinosaur hand puppets, and re-purposed *Carnosaur* footage. (In a dumbfounding sop to plausibility, they actually provide an explanation as to how these prehistoric creatures can still be alive: it seems the water on this island has Fountain of Youth-style properties. Thanks, movie, that really was my only question.) Dumb jokes, lots of tits, embarrassing special effects, and lines like "Die, you dinosaur dick!" ensue. In the end the soldiers defeat enough dinosaurs to earn a place in the tribe, but instead of going on a well-earned fuck-frenzy most of them opt to get married to a single cavegirl! So, given the eternal youth, this means that they will *literally* be married to the same woman *forever*. It's a pretty horrific ending to an otherwise lighthearted boobie adventure, that's for sure.

Dinosaur Island

(2002)

Directed by Will Meugniot

The company that produced this cartoon, The Incredible World of Dick, is infamous for developing or licensing cool concepts and then bumble-fucking the vast majority of them. Fortunately, this one-off movie isn't too bad. Four kids are cast in a ripoff of *Survivor* only to have their plane crash en route, stranding them on an uncharted island (because those still exist) populated by dinosaurs (ditto). Oh, wait, it's actually an inaccessible *mesa* populated by dinosaurs. So why is this movie called "Dinosaur Island"? Fucking idiots. That aside the characters are likable enough, the dialogue is occasionally clever, and let's face it, cartoon dinosaurs are almost always cool, as long as they're interacting with other cartoons and not real actors. Of course some dumb and/ or lazy shit does slip through (people riding dinosaurs; cavemen so flailingly terrified and intimidated by technology that you'd think they worked in legacy publishing; the kids' escape from Dinosaur ~~Island~~ Mesa is far too abrupt and convenient), but the story is solid enough that even when the kids inevitably learn to work together it feels natural and organic, instead of being some obligatory lesson the writer was compelled to cram down our throats. Overall, one of the better productions The Incredible World of Dick has ejaculated into our collected eyeballs.

The Dinosaur Project

(2012)

"Directed" by Sid Bennett

Being too cheap to buy a tripod has somehow become an acceptable filmmaking "technique", and while this lost & found footage "movie" (sporting a title that is in no way reminiscent of *The Blair Witch Project*) (fucking duh) obviously wants to ape that non-style's "success" it falls back on standard Lost World cliches almost immediately as our heroes helicopter is brought down by pterodactyls while flying over Africa. Soon more dinosaurs come crawling out of the woodwork, and eventually our cast is sucked into a Lost World proper in much the same manner as the family in *Valley of the Dinosaurs*, a very silly Saturday morning cartoon produced for children that is nevertheless superior to this movie in every quantifiable way. The main kid is incredibly annoying (did it not dawn on these clowns that annoying children are a huge part of what's wrong with the movie that was most likely their primary inspiration, the original *Jurassic Park*?); the sole hottie is eaten first (her exceptional ass was sorely missed for the remainder of the running time); and the end is just a high-tech take on the end of *The Land That Time Forgot* (1975), a movie that – this is becoming a running theme here – is infinitely superior to *The Dinosaur Project* in every way. Oh, and let's not forget that *The Dinosaur Project* is a lost & found footage movie, with all the disdain that this automatically warrants. "Crafting" a lost & found footage movie makes you a "filmmaker" about as much as changing the radio station makes you a musician. Fuck this irrelevant garbage. It doesn't even qualify.

Dinosaurs and the Bible

(2003)

Dr. Kent Hovind

This goddamned DVD is *two hours and thirty-seven minutes long*. Why oh why can't crazy people ever be succinct?

Fundamental Christians have a weird relationship with dinosaurs. Some of them claim that all dinosaur fossils are fakes, planted by God to test our faith. (Why God would want to trick us into not believing in him and then damn us to Hell forever for the crime is never explained. He works in mysterious, dickish ways.) Other fundies think that dinosaurs did exist, but drowned during Noah's flood, and still others insist that dinosaurs were created by the Devil, just like alcohol, rock music, and Miley Cyrus. (Utterly ridiculous. Miley Cyrus was obviously created in Heaven.) Dr. Kent Hovind (currently in jail for non-dinosaur-related crimes) has no doubt that dinosaurs existed; according to him the Garden of Eden was a regular Jurassic Park, and there *were* dinosaurs on Noah's ark (little ones, obviously). So where are they now? The easy answer would be Dinosaur Island, but according to Kent what really happened was that they reinvented themselves as honest-to-fuck fire-breathing dragons, only to eventually be hunted to near-extinction. In fact, in one of the lesser-known books of the Bible Daniel himself (star of the Book of Daniel) personally explodes a dragon by tricking it into eating pitch, and could someone please tell me why the story of Noah was tapped for a Hollywood blockbuster before this was?

So despite what Science (*snort*) tells us, dinosaurs hung on forever, fighting Indians, attacking old-timey mariners, and just generally raising hell in the margins of history. And they're still around today! In fact, a generous portion of this guy's presentation is a lengthy examination of modern-day lake monster/sea serpent/dinosaur sightings, featuring interviews with witnesses, rare news clips, and so on, dating all the way back to *1980*. Trust me, if you're into cryptozoology (defined as the study of gullibility) you'll eat this shit up.

All of this is, at worst, only moderately insane, but it's only a matter of time before Kent goes entirely off the rails. He claims that the Devil wants to "use dinosaurs against God". (Seriously, this cat is just full of blockbuster movies.) He says that the theory of evolution is part of a New World Order conspiracy perpetrated by liberals, the public school system, and our museums. And, worst of all, he seriously suggests creating a Christian version of Barney (the purple dinosaur) to teach children about Jesus. Of course he wraps it all up by assuring us that every single person watching this DVD – every single person on Earth, in fact – deserves to die and go to Hell. Which, by definition, includes the President of the United States. That's right, he just threatened the President. Secret Service, do your duty.

Dinosaurs "Changing Nature"

(1994)

Written by Kirk Thatcher

The 1990s were a terrible decade for popular culture, almost as bad as the 1970s, or the 1530s. Hair metal dodged irrelevance by disguising itself as "grunge", "fashion" consisted mostly of flannel shirts and scowling, and with very few exceptions television was even more of a wasteland than usual. Only in the early 1990s, when drugs were super prevalent but also kind of shitty, could a show as brazenly worthless as *Dinosaurs* be successful, coasting entirely on bright colors and barely-jokes crafted expressly for the sub-retarded. (Submitted as Exhibit B: *Friends*.) You remember *Dinosaurs*, right? Here's a reminder: "I'm the baby! Gotta love me!" Yeah, that's the one. "I'm the baby!" Fuck you, you little pink cunt nugget. *Dinosaurs* was everything wrong with sitcoms times ten, serving up the same reheated turds that were already groan-inducing cliches when *I Love Lucy* trotted them out in the 1920s or whatever, only this time perpetrated by humanoid dinosaurs. This shit program did get one thing right though, both scientifically and ethically: in the final episode, *all the dinosaurs fucking died*. Maybe you vaguely remember this but think it was your imagination. Nope, it really happened. It all starts (to end) when the main dinosaur – your typical fat, dumb, lazy sitcom dad à la every TV show ever – wants to get rid of some troublesome weeds. He spearheads the worldwide spraying of a new defoliant that ends up devastating the entire planet, kicking off a chain of events that eventually leads to an ice age, sealing the fate of his entire species. Including the fucking baby. And rest assured I'm not extrapolating here: the closing moments of this episode make it irrefutably clear that the dinosaurs are doomed; utterly, gloriously doomed. I'm calling it right now: best series finale *ever*.

Interesting side note: the script for this episode was once re-purposed as an episode of *King of Queens*. Except that version started with the husband wiping out all plant life on Earth by farting, while in the B story I fucked his wife. CBS rejected the proposal though, plus told me to stop sending them scripts or they'd get a restraining order.

Dinosaurus!

(1960)

Directed by Irvin S. Yeaworth, Jr.

There's nothing like a good dinosaur rampage; even when the dinosaur is just a puppet or a guy in a ratty suit it's generally pretty entertaining. This movie pisses it all up though. Some construction guys are exploding things when they unearth two *Land of the Lost*-looking dinosaurs and a caveman. Of course they all come back to life, but unfortunately only one of the dinosaurs starts killing people; the other one just lumbers about for a while and then befriends this annoying little kid. The kid even rides the damn thing around! You have *got* to me shitting me. It looks like they might finally kick the action up a notch when the caveman gets his hands on an axe, but he doesn't ice anybody either; he just runs around engaging in zany slapstick antics, like trying to eat the ceramic fruit and whatnot. At one point he even hits someone in the face with a pie! Ha ha! It's comedy! You stupid assholes. Papa's got a brand new shit bag, and it's called *Dinosaurus!* Fucking weak.

Dino Squad

(2002)

Produced by The Incredible World of Dick

Not to be confused with 1997's *Extreme Dinosaurs*, which was basically the same show, *Dino Squad* begins when five detestable teenage asswipes ("I'm not here to be the poster boy for cooperation," says one, after being asked to simply not be a dick) gain the power to turn into dinosaurs after being exposed to DNA-mutating ooze. Because, you know, the Teenage Mutant Ninja Turtles. (Seriously, if you can watch garbage like this and *Street Sharks* and not agree that the Teenage Mutant Ninja Turtles were the worst thing to ever happen to cartoons, you're only deluding yourself.) Fortunately, the kids' biology teacher just *happens* to be a 65-million-year-old Velociraptor that has ESP, can take human form, and, at some point, earned a degree in secondary education. Best of all, she has enough bread squirreled away to finance all sorts of super-gizmos for the kids, including DNA-altering beam weapons and modded-out dinosaur-themed motorcycles. (Hey, even at the shittiest rate available, your savings account will build up a lot of interest over 65 million years.) Under her tutelage the kids use their amazing abilities to fight crime and learn valuable lessons, like how to deal with bullies. (Their advice: don't stand up to a bully, because eventually a snake will fall on him, magically turning him into your friend. And yes, most of this show's plots *do* sound like a list of random words strung together.) *Dino Squad* is dumb as fuck and an insult to all but the stupidest children, so hey, maybe yours will like it. Me, I've got better things to do. Okay, fine, I don't. Fuck you.

Dino World!

(1998)

Kids@Discovery Series

I had no intention of covering any (legitimate) dinosaur documentaries here, because there are entirely too many of them to even scratch the surface and besides I didn't want this book polluted with a bunch of facts. I decided to make an exception for this one though, because, first off, it's aimed at very young children, and the misinformation Them likes to feed little kids can be extraordinary. Then there was this gem, from the back of the DVD case:

"Learn about different types of dinosaurs and how they lived, and the debate behind what caused dino extinction. Was it a dinosaur war...?"

What??? A "dinosaur war"? Who's been slinging *that* theory around, and why don't they have their own series on the History Channel yet? The hostess is a grownup named Teresa Roncon, who some people (Canadians) may remember as a Canadian VJ for whatever used to pass for Canadian MTV, probably something with a Maple Leaf in the title. She's pretty hot; I would totally hit that in the museum restroom while the kids were out on the sales floor, learning about dinosaurs. (Yes, the *sales floor*. Because everyone is always selling something.) She's the only good thing about this debacle though. It's jam-packed with seizure-inducing flashing lights and spazmo graphics, all in a failed attempt to hide the fact that it's basically just a goony, over-enthusiastic German guy talking about skeletons while the hostess tries (unsuccessfully) not to laugh at him. Oh, and to eat up the generous running time (20 minutes) they occasionally ask random children stupid questions and let them ramble incoherently for a while. The only way this presentation could be any more slight is if it was just a graphic reading "Dinosaurs are kewl!" Oh, and they only mention the "dinosaur war" long enough to point out what a stupid theory it is. Thanks a lot, DVD case. I came for the crazy, and instead I got a bunch of dull, flatly-presented facts and a closing segment that's *a three-minute advertisement for a toy*. Of course, I'm a grownup. The important thing is, will this DVD get your kids excited about dinosaurs? I think the part where they're discussing paleontology as a career best answers *that* question:

HOSTESS: "Do you know what you want to be when you grow up?"

KID: "Yes. A lawyer."

Dunston Checks In

(1996)

Directed by Ken Kwapis

Note: This serves as my review for every god-awful slapstick monkey comedy ever made. Suck my dick, Hollywood. Of the hundreds of miserable, soul-crushing choices available, I selected this one because at least they had the decency to eschew a terrible play-on-words title like "Going Ape" or "MVP: Most Valuable Primate".

The three things all Hollywood executives are convinced are funny: farting, cross-dressing, and monkeys. If you could make a movie that was entirely about monkeys in dresses farting, every producer in Hollywood would shit themselves with joy and then go blind masturbating to it.

So, these two brothers live in a hotel with their manager dad, à la *The Suite Life of Zack & Cody*. (At least, I assume that was the premise of that show. The only Disney Channel shows I actually watch are the ones with hot teenage chickies as the headliners.) After they pull a prank that results in guests being sprayed with water, a small dog flying through the air, and a fat woman falling into a fountain (I have to admit; well done) their dad (George Costanza) gives them an ultimatum: straighten up, or there will be... no consequences, actually, because apparently he's a huge pussy. Not long after a jewel thief checks in with his trained orangutan, Dunston. Dunston runs away though, so now he's loose in the hotel, engaging in antics. He drinks out of the toilet (because he eats shit); assaults several people (because he's a violent, dangerous animal that should be put to sleep); and steals just about everything, except my heart because, seriously, fuck this movie. When the two brothers discover Dunston, they immediately inform a grownup, the monkey is quickly taken into custody, and their dad congratulates them on their new-found sense of responsibility. Ha ha! *Of course* I'm fucking kidding. Actually, they rent the monkey his own room under a fake name, which the three of them proceed to thoroughly trash while shamelessly stealing from the hotel. Our heroes, ladies and gentlemen. Eventually Pee-wee Herman is called in to deal with the monkey, and he turns out to be hilariously dangerous/crazy so that's one bright spot, at least. His deranged speech confusing pet Easter rabbits with flushed baby alligators and/or orangutans is definitely the high point of the movie, not that that's saying much. Another high point: Dunston gets hurt, there's a little blood, and for one brief moment I thought the frowny-faced asshole might actually be dead. Okay, fine, I knew better, but it was a beautiful fantasy nonetheless. For the most part though, this flick is just an endless parade of retarded idiocy. There's a food fight... people are accidentally shot with tranquilizer darts... uptight women fall into large cakes... and so on and so forth. In fact, calling it "retarded" is probably an insult to the legitimately retarded, since even those pudding-hurlers wouldn't be entertained by this slack-jawed drivel. Look, I know this movie is meant for children, but even children don't like to be talked down to. And trust me, they notice when a small dog impossibly survives a fall from a hotel roof, or when the jazz band at a swanky party is clearly jamming its heart out but some fucknut in post *forgot to dub in any music*. That's right, this production is so shoddy that it can't even live up to the universally low expectations of a monkey fart comedy. Good job, team! I'll bet your mothers are proud.

Proposed sequel: "Dunston Checks Out". In a hail of bullets, preferably.

The Eden Formula

(2006)

Directed by John Carl Buechler

Since *Jurassic Park* showed us the way, people in the movies have been cooking up live dinosaurs like the people at your office brew pots of coffee. And, despite the innumerable species of tiny dinosaurs that existed, they always decide to whip up a T. rex. Doesn't anyone remember that little poem from inside our 1970s lunchboxes, the one that started "Safety first is an important rule..."?

This particular T. rex gets pretty angry when a fat guy teases it with some Arby's, so the fat guy is the first to go after it gets loose. The dinosaur quickly breaks out of the facility where it's being held (courtesy re-used footage from one of the *Carnosaur* movies), wanders the streets for a while, comes back when the people at the facility literally ring the dinner bell, leaves again, wanders around the neighborhood, unnoticed, in broad daylight, and finally returns to the facility yet again for the big finale, which involves exploding radios and random violence perpetrated on the vending machine delivery guy. This flick is so cobbled-together that when E.T.'s mom flees in a police car at one point, all the long shots show a male police officer in full uniform actually driving the car. Of course they're lucky there are any cops near the scene at all: local law enforcement is apparently stretched so thin that the dispatch officer is forced to double as the desk sergeant *and* the sole 911 operator for the entire city, although he could use some additional training in the latter: "Nine-one-one emergency. Can I direct your call?" he says when he answers the line. Yeah, direct it to nine-one-one, you fucking idiot. Like a lot of cost-efficient, crap movies, *mucho* time is spent walking around in corridors and talking tough, plus one painfully extended sequence is included just to to set up a terrible "dino-SORE" pun. And the endlessly-recycled scene of a ninja grabbing the steering wheel from someone and driving their car into an electrical transformer, where it explodes (previously seen in movies as diverse and shitty as *Sorceress II: The Temptress* and *976-EVIL II*), shows up here, too. In the end, the main guy recklessly blows up an entire office building to kill the dinosaur, never mind that a) the dinosaur wasn't even in this building, it was in the parking lot and b) there was a hottie inside that blast zone, goddammit. Sure, she was one of the bad guys, but so what? Hotness knows no moral compass.

Encino Man

(1992)

Directed by Les Mayfield

Every single thing about Pauly Shore is the worst possible example of the thing in question: his irritating voice, his awful hair, his dopey fucking face, and especially his miserable stoner-meets-PKU-baby shtick. I swear, if God had known Pauly Shore would be the end result when he created Adam and ~~Lilith~~ Eve, he probably would have made lizard people instead. This flick came out at a time when Pauly Shore was briefly, inexplicably popular (thanks a lot, America), but even fart-obsessed Hollywood wasn't delusional enough (yet) to cast him in a leading role. Instead, he's the "zany sidekick", while the main guy is played by a dork who's name I never did catch and who I can't recall ever seeing again. Technically making him, I guess, *a less successful actor than Pauly Shore*. Now that's depressing. [Addendum: Apparently I was wrong, because he was in *The Lord of the Rings* (2001-2003). Who knew?]

So anyway, Pauly and the main guy ("Pauly and the Main Guy" sounds like it should be the name of a failed 1970s sitcom) unearth a caveman in the latter's back yard, and after the requisite scene where the caveman freaks out and destroys everything, they clean him up and take him to school, where they pass him off as a foreign exchange student, or a robot, or something. And before you can remember which one was the Molly Ringwald and which one was the Smurf (hint: Molly Ringwald is the one you want to fuck), a modicum of coolness is achieved, the bully is defeated, the main guy gets the girl, and a valuable lesson is learned by all. Except of course Hollywood, who proceeded to cast Pauly Shore in several more movies. *Encino Man* is clearly a 1980s flick made during that brief period when the 1980s bled over into the 1990s: the hair is completely '80s, the fashions are completely '80s, the music is completely '80s (Def Leppard, some other shitty bands that sound kinda like Def Leppard), and with only minor tweaks the script could have easily served as *Teen Wolf 3* or even a John Hughes movie, if John Hughes had suffered recent head trauma.

Utterly pointless, but it does feature an early appearance by mega-goddess Rose McGowan, whose next role would be "Amy Blue" in *The Doom Generation* (1995). That's right; this poor, poor girl went on to a project that was actually *worse* than *Encino Man*.

The Extraordinary Adventures of Adèle Blanc-Sec

(2010)

Directed by Luc Besson

If you've read a lot of Franco-European adventure comics in the original French (and who hasn't?) you're probably familiar with Adèle Blanc-Sec, and while her comic books are mediocre at best they're a *Classic Comics* adaptation of Shakespeare compared to this fuck-awful movie, which tries to cram approximately sixteen different Adèle adventures into one story and ends up being a hopeless hodge-podge of lunacy that starts with a guy using ESP to bring a killer pterodactyl to life and ends with an army of friendly mummies strolling around Paris, taking in the sights. You'd think the middle would be primarily concerned with getting us from point A (ESP pterodactyl) to point B (benign mummy invasion), no easy task. But nope. Instead, it's made up of slapstick horseshit, a cute little dog befriending the pterodactyl like this was an especially ill-conceived Disney movie, absurdly out-of-place pathos involving Adèle's sister and her accidental lobotomy-via-hatpin, and Adèle riding the pterodactyl to the rescue when a peripheral character is about to be hanged. And I'd just like to say for the record that a good fifteen minutes before the latter actually occurred I thought to myself "I'll bet she's going to end up riding that pterodactyl around. God damn this stupid fucking movie." When even your movie's most outrageous/idiotic elements are effortlessly predictable, you've failed on every level imaginable and some that haven't even been invented yet, although after analyzing this flick supercomputers are currently working on it and hope to identify and quantify many more ways to fail in the future, in case they make a sequel. In the meantime, fuck this movie, fuck Adèle (I'll handle that bit of business myself. She is pretty hot.), and fuck the French for being too busy smoking cigarettes to stop this terrible film from happening. *Vous êtes tous des crétins.* Assholes.

The Flintstones in Viva Rock Vegas

(2000)

Directed by Brian Levant

Making a live-action movie based on *The Flintstones* – a terrible, unfunny cartoon structured entirely around rock puns, that has nevertheless become a major cultural touchstone because our culture sucks – is bad enough. But the fact that it made enough money for them to bowel movement out this brain-raping sequel is nobody's fault but your own, moviegoers. Hang you heads in shame. *Hang your heads in shame.* Of course one of the first jokes is a dinosaur farting, and this movie is so fucking uninspired that there's even a pie-in-the-face gag, a bit that director Buster Keaton considered unacceptably hackneyed in *1923*. All told there's only one legitimate laugh in this entire, miserable exercise ("How old did you say you were?"), but, in the end, the biggest problem is the cast. Astoundingly, the main actor is completely incapable of playing Fred Flintstone, one of the least-nuanced characters in television history. Seriously, the only thing easier to play would be one of the rocks. And yet, somehow, this guy is so flat and unlikable as Fred Flintstone that they would've been better off using a cardboard cutout. The guy playing Barney Rubble is almost as bad, but Barney has the benefit of being as pointless to this story as he was on the cartoon, so not noticing him is kind of appropriate. And to be fair, the actor playing Barney gives the impression that he's a slack-jawed dipshit in real life too, so decent casting here, I guess. [Addendum: According to the credits, Barney is played by Stephen Baldwin, so it looks like I was right.] As for the girls, well, the woman(?) playing Wilma is just straight-up hideous, but Betty is pretty goddamned hot, and actually does an okay job. So congratulations, Jane Krakowski, for being the sole reason to sit through *The Flintstones in Viva Rock Vegas*. There's something to put on your tombstone. Worst of all though is the producers' decision to include Fred and Barney's space alien friend, the Great Gazoo, and it doesn't help that they made him look like a creepy old man/chronic masturbator/child molester. Still, this kind of makes sense, since, as he explains, he's on Earth to "observe mating rituals", i.e. to watch people fuck. The slight plot, clearly an afterthought, concerns how Fred and Barney landed their future wives, Wilma and Betty.

So that's the premise - two dumb assholes try to score with a hot chick and a post-op tranny, while a pervert from outer space spies on them. Family entertainment, everybody! Naturally the featured dinosaurs are especially cheap-looking cartoons, but it's hard to criticize this seeing as this movie is, well, based on an especially cheap-looking cartoon. In fact, this movie breaks out a lot of gimmicks/effects that tend to be exclusive to cartoons, like Fred "shrinking" when he's made to feel small. Which buggers the question, why even make a live-action movie of this material at all? I mean really, is it just to piss intelligent people off?

Flying Monkeys

(2013)

Directed by Robert Grasmere

"Welcome to Gale, Kansas". You mean like Dorothy Gale, from *The Wizard of Oz*? This movie is SO WITTY. Look, the flying cartoon monkeys appear in the very first scene so we already know they look like shit, and within the first couple of minutes you've swiped the most famous line from *Dazed and Confused* (1993). It's painfully obvious that you're operating on zero talent here and are reduced to references and stealing, so could you stop trying to be clever, you sub-talented fucks, and just bring on the gore and tits?

So why are there flying monkeys? Well, at first there's only one (as if that explains anything), which our main guy foolishly buys his daughter as a pet. (Monkeys aren't pets, as *Conquest of the Planet of the Apes* should have taught us.) At this point it looks like a regular monkey, but before the daughter can so much as get it fitted for its little tuxedo (can't have a monkey serving you drinks if it's not wearing a tuxedo) it's transmogrifying into a flying monster and killing people. First to be snuffed: the daughter's boyfriend, who was previously pretty vocal in his displeasure re: competing with the monkey for her affections. (I'm not even gonna try to follow his disturbing train of thought here. But a quick online search confirms that there is indeed porn of it.) And it's about to get worse: it seems our magical, flying monkey spawns additional monkeys whenever it gets ~~wet~~ killed, and since most people's immediate reaction to killer monkeys is to shoot them (or, if my recent online research is any indication, fuck them), pretty soon there's dozens, maybe hundreds, of flying monkeys on the rampage. (I briefly considered pausing a shot of the monkeys swarming above the city and counting them so I could provide a more concrete number, but there's such a thing as caring too much about your work, and I decided that doing this would've crossed that line.) So, basically, this movie is one part *Gremlins*, one part stool-hurling, and all parts terrible, full of shitty acting, obnoxious characters, and no tits. Even the chicks are below average, probably the producer's niece and her dingbat sorority sisters or something. Fly, monkeys, fly! And don't come back!

Galaxy of the Dinosaurs

(1992)

Directed by Lance Randas

After an intro admitting what a piece of shit this movie is (points for honesty), our story proper begins, and while this is clearly backyard cinema the main chick is a damn fine sight so I figured I'd give it a chance. Okay, movie, you have one hour to impress me. Go!

Our "heroes" are five aliens, or, more accurately, five regular people that this movie assures us are aliens. Frankly they look more like refugee "types" from a shitty college comedy, including a "funny" fat guy wearing a Hawaiian shirt and a lei. Do they even have Hawaii in space? Regardless, they're on their way to lunch when their spaceship crash-lands on a planet crawling with dinosaurs. "We're stuck on this planet... we're not getting off!" exclaims one guy. (Not true. I got off every time the main chick was on-screen.) The main chick is bum-rushed by a spider of indeterminate size; everyone eats hallucinogenic mushrooms; a dude cracks wise while being carried off to his death by a T. rex; no one questions why the caveman they encounter is wearing slacks and a dress shirt; the fat guy kills and eats an entire Brontosaurus (it's comedy!); telephone poles are occasionally visible in the background; and the end rips off *Planet of the Apes* (1968), but with a humorous twist. And by "humorous", of course, I mean "fairly annoying".

The dinosaur effects are all stolen from the criminally-underrated classic *Planet of Dinosaurs* (1977), so naturally the dinosaurs and the actors never appear together in the same shot. Hell, they don't even seem to exist in the same ecosystem - the actors are in the woods behind a strip mall or something, while the dinosaurs are clearly in the desert. It's like you're watching two different movies simultaneously: *Planet of Dinosaurs*, and a shitty one your drunk, talentless friends shot with a circa-1992 consumer-grade camera, just before going home to fuck their own mothers. It's a complete bucket of shit.

Oh well, at least the main chick was hot.

Gamera: The Guardian of the Universe

(1995)

Directed by Shûsuke Kaneko

In case you're one of those people who has absolutely no idea what's going on, Gamera was a giant, flying turtle that spent the latter half of the 1960s rescuing obnoxious Japanese children from sexy female aliens. (I generally rooted for the aliens.) His movies were so successful that the studio that produced them went bankrupt, but in 1995 someone decided that he was ripe for a reboot. A lot of people eschewed recreational drug use during the "Just Say No" 1980s, but drugs had become pretty popular again by 1995. I don't think this is a coincidence.

Giant bats appear, because Japan, eating people and destroying everything. Shortly thereafter, Gamera shows up, provoking even more anxiety. ("Will it attack Tokyo?" one chick asks. You naïve bitch.) Still, at least their bat problem seems to be solved when Gamera hilariously blows one of the bats to pieces with his fiery breath. Unfortunately, the remaining bat grows even larger; large enough, in fact, to give Gamera more than a run for his money. Gamera's solution? Absorb energy from a cute teenage girl until he's powerful enough to prevail. That's right; Gamera, the "guardian of the universe", has to tag out to a *fifteen-year-old girl*. No wonder his movies aren't as popular as Godzilla's.

Ganjasaurus Rex

(1987)

Directed by Ursi Reynolds

These hippie weeders (with names like "Moss" and "Cloud" and "Assface") (fine, I made that last one up) have developed a gigantic marijuana plant dubbed *cannabis sequoia*, and their mostly unfunny antics take up the first third of this movie, once again driving home the fact that, while things are often funnier *when* you're smoking pot, *pot itself is not intrinsically funny*. I know "What if Godzilla smoked pot?" sounded hilarious when you were toking up in Dylan's basement, but in the light of day, $2314 later, as a real movie (well, sort of) that it took eleven (eleven!) people to write, it's exactly as terrible as any non-stoned person could have easily predicted. Their version of Godzilla (and yes, this flick does its non-actionable best to imply that "Ganjasaurus Rex" is, in fact, Godzilla himself) is realized via some sort of unclassifiable shit-mation; the "heroes" are unlikable, sub-slapstick idiots; and the movie's sole hottie dances around in a field at one point but never gets naked. Fucking hippies. I did appreciate the reference to McDonald's late, lamented McDLT sandwich though. Who doesn't miss the McDLT, with its outrageous, double-sized styrofoam packaging that disregarded any and all environmental concerns in its aim to keep the hot side hot and the cool side cool? They brought it back for a while (sans the ostentatious packaging) as the "Big n' Tasty", but that's gone now too and I've essentially renounced McDonald's ever since. Down with the clown!

Anyway, there's barely enough material here to fuel a particularly-uninspired *Saturday Night Live* sketch (like from one of the weaker *SNL* eras, say 1975-Present), but, to be fair, there are one or two passable gags, and at least when the script called for a helicopter they were able to afford/steal some footage of an actual helicopter, trumping several Syphilis Channel movies I could mention. In the end, the best you can say about *Ganjasaurus Rex* is that, while horrible, it's nowhere near as bad as it could have been. Of course, technically, you could say that about the Third Reich too.

Prediction: This movie will eventually be remade starring Seth Rogen.

Gappa: The Triphibian Monsters

(1967)

Directed by Haruyasu Noguchi

So... "gappa" is the plural, then? If I'm gonna write about them I really need to know.

These nips on the hunt for exotic animals hit the jackpot when they discover a baby gappa, a giant lizard that someone in the party would have undoubtedly claimed was "supposed to be extinct" if any of them knew what it was. Of course they take it back to Japan, and of course mom and dad gappa come looking for it, and of course by the time it's all over everyone's insurance rates will have gone up by at least 2000%. The first act of most giant monster movies is generally pretty boring, but there's actually some good stuff here before we get to the primary action, including a crazy-looking bird puppet, a cool underground lake, this neat strobe effect before the monsters pop out of the water, and classic lines like this:

CHICK: "I'm scared! I don't like places like this!"

DUDE: "Don't be silly. You're supposed to be a news photographer!"

CHICK: "But..."

DUDE: "Then go back to Tokyo and learn to cook."

(Ha ha! It's funny because he's sexist.) (He's not wrong though.)

And this:

GUY WHO'S UNCLEAR ON THE CONCEPT: "But even the impossible can happen."

Obviously the success of any giant monster flick is measured in property damage, and once the gappa make land they do a fair job of busting up the joint, but it's nothing we haven't seen before and frankly it's a lot more fun – and forgivable – when Godzilla does it. Because we know him. In the end the gappa are just too damn generic, and there's not enough to set them apart from a hundred other monsters on the waiting list to destroy Tokyo.

Gargantua

(1998)

Directed by Bradford May

(Note to nit-picky idiots who will undoubtedly e-mail me about this: Technically, the monsters in *Gargantua* are mutated aquatic salamanders, not dinosaurs. But if it walks like a dinosaur, and it talks like a dinosaur, and it's too late for me to include this movie in my sharks-and-sea-monsters book, then I'm calling it a dinosaur.)

Noted Internet misogynist Jayne Cobb, in his pre-*Firefly* days, is a marine biologist investigating several mysterious deaths-by-monster. Meanwhile, his unsupervised child befriends the baby version (which looks like a goddamned free-with-your-kids'-meal hand puppet) and spends an entire *day* just sitting there, watching it frolic around. Jesus Christ, somebody get this kid an X-Box. Soon a much larger monster (a somewhat more sophisticated puppet) strolls out of the surf and starts nomming on folks, and everyone assumes that monster #2 is the adult version until a *third* monster, considerably bigger than the second (a guy inside a puppet?), appears to do the town Godzilla style. (In sci-fi/ horror terms, this sort of escalation is known as a "wait until Charlie comes", or, alternately, a "double Gorgo".) Needless to say, I wasn't exactly blindsided when a fourth monster subsequently showed up. (Now it's a triple Gorgo.) The setting is fun (a microscopic island nation where the president doubles as the bartender), and the old-school special effects are charming (in this context, that means "bad"), but there's no gore, no tits, and the end is the worst kind of heavy-handed, family-centric horseshit, with a closing line that literally made me puke. And I do mean literally. It's okay, though; the dog licked most of it up.

The Ghost of Slumber Mountain

(1918)

Produced by Herbert M. Dawley

This movie is silent, which is probably for the best since the person who wrote is all but illiterate. "Please 'Unk' tell us a really truly story about wild animals er sumpin." says one title card. The tale "Unk" ("The Unk of Fuck", they used to call him.) (Well they should have.) tells concerns the time he climbed Slumber Mountain with his buddy and then tried to convince the guy to strip naked and prance around like a baby deer so he could paint a picture of him doing this despicably perverted thing. And no I am not misinterpreting the situation or making some weird, impenetrable joke; that's really what happens in this movie. Next the two of them go looking for "Mad Dick" (again, I'm not kidding) while the buddy recalls the time he saw ol' Dick checking out something with a "queer instrument", or what non-perverts might call a "telescope". And no I don't want to deep-throat the telescope or shove it up my ass or anything of the sort, so don't even ask, movie. That night our main guy falls asleep by the fire thinking about Dick (of course he does), only to be "aroused" (not "roused", AROUSED) some time later. What are the chances that it's Mad Dick, arousing him with his queer instrument? Shamelessly breaking into Dick's cabin, he finds the telescope, which, upon closer inspection, looks more like a View-Master. This probably helps to explain what happens next: looking through the View-Master, he sees live dinosaurs! And I have to say, for 19 fucking 18 the special effects here are pretty... You know what, never mind - I'm not gonna bullshit you. The special effects suck. But hey, it was 1918, what the hell do you want? Anyway, our main guy watches the dinosaurs for a while until, suddenly, one of them comes after him, somehow. (He previously emphasized that the dinosaurs were "<u>far far away</u>," so maybe he was looking through the telescope backwards or something.) He runs for it, only to wake up by the fire because IT WAS ALL A DREAM. Are you fucking kidding me? I'm sorry, but even in 1918 "it was all a dream" was a shockingly unsophisticated cinematic cop-out, and back then there were entire movies being made about spraying people in the face with a seltzer bottle.

The Ghost of Slumber Mountain is historically important (probably), but as we all know "important" is almost never the same as "entertaining". Still, with several minutes allegedly missing (good) it is tolerably short, and it's really not stupid enough to piss anybody off, so as far as I'm concerned it has plenty of current movies beat by a Hollywood mile. I mean seriously, *Paul Blart: Mall Cop 2*? Get bent.

Godzilla Raids Again

(1955)

Directed by Motoyoshi Oda

Did you ever read the Star Wars novel *Splinter of the Mind's Eye*? It's basically the shitty, first draft of *The Empire Strikes Back* and would have been George Lucas's go-to if *Star Wars* (1977) had tanked at the box office; a cheap, single-location sequel that would allow him to play around in that universe one final time before he was reduced to directing episodes of *Laverne & Shirley* and eventually killing himself. Well, apparently this is the Godzilla universe parallel, because even though it's the official sequel to the original *Godzilla* (1954) it's unusually short, slapdash as hell, and padded with stock footage, filler, and clips from other movies, all barely held together with monotonous, racist narration ("Though our city is in frames..."). There's so much disconnect from the original that *Godzilla is never even referred to by name*. The monster fights are slapsticky and ridiculous, even by the generally low standards of an old-school Godzilla movie, and his spiky, Ankylosaurus-looking opponent is saddled with the cumbersome, overwrought moniker "Anguilasaurus: Killer of the Living". Seriously, could you maybe rein in the hyperbole a little bit? It's a shame, because I really like Anguirus, as he later came to be called. For a while, I even had a toy version of him. I had to get rid of it though, because my ex-girlfriend's pet hedgehog kept trying to mate with it.

Godzilla's Revenge

(1969)

Directed by Ishirô Honda

There sure are a lot of Godzilla movies, a neophyte might think. *I wonder which one is the worst?* Well, here's the ass-reaming answer. This annoying little kid who's fascinated with monsters and burned-out vacuum tubes is tormented by a bully named "Gabara". (Sounds suspiciously like "Gamera", Godzilla's rival series). Later, he's kidnapped by and ultimately Home Alones some slapsticky crooks responsible for the theft of fifty million yen. (Holy shit! Wait a minute, that's only like three hundred bucks.) As a result of this misadventure, he learns that fighting is the best policy and then plays a cruel, dangerous prank on a complete stranger, winning the bully's admiration. The end. If it sounds like there's something missing from this synopsis, you're right. Godzilla plays no part in the action whatsoever, except in the main kid's imagination, where he regularly visits Monster Island, or, more accurately, where he remembers all the Godzilla movies he's seen previously since that's where most of this movie's monster footage comes from. While (not really) on Monster Island he imaginary-befriends Minya (the Scrappy-Doo of the Godzilla universe), who looks like a cross between the Pillsbury Doughboy and an animated pile of shit and sounds like McDonaldland's Grimace, if Grimace were mildly retarded. Okay, fine, fully retarded. It's kind of like *Calvin & Hobbes*, except Japanese and terrible, and even the tacked-on monster fights are recycled garbage, like the bit where Godzilla plays volleyball with a giant lobster. He should've kicked that fucking lobster right back into the drink, boiled it to death with his atomic breath, and then served it with a baseball stadium full of melted butter on the side. That would've been delicious.

Godzilla vs. Mechagodzilla II

(1993)

Directed by Takao Okawara

Ah, hell, I thought this was *Godzilla vs. Mechagodzilla Part One*. I hope I don't have too much trouble following the plot. Ha ha ha ha ha ha ha! And subtitles? Seriously? Because the original, Japanese acting in Godzilla movies is so nuanced that you just have to preserve it? (Then again, subtitled movies have always been considered kind of high-brow, whereas Godzilla movies are generally considered to be low-brow, so maybe this is just an attempt to even things out.) At any rate, the Godzilla series has had more reboots and proposed more alternate futures than any given six months of X-Men comics, so where this one falls in the long-standing Godzilla-Mechagodzilla feud is anyone's guess. What I find far, far more interesting (and I'm sure Perez Hilton would agree with me, if he wasn't too busy sucking AIDS out of a mule's dick) is the fact that, at some point, *Godzilla apparently knocked up Rodan*. How else do you explain the fact that they're both so eager to claim full custody when a baby Godzilla suddenly appears? This, of course, leads to the mother (heh) of all fights between the two, followed by several more awesome/hilarious bouts including Godzilla vs. Mechagodzilla, Rodan vs.

Mechagodzilla, and finally Godzilla and Rodan vs. Mechagodzilla with Garuda Backpack Accessory. High points include the part where Rodan tries to peck Godzilla's face off so he unapologetically chokes that bitch out, and the part where Godzilla trashes the city of Kyoto (which is just "Tokyo" spelled sideways). Flaws include the fact that everyone in this movie seems to have ESP (which is both retarded and completely unnecessary); the monsters breaking out some of the same ridiculous pro-wrestling moves that they used in the 1970s; and the American scientist with the beard, who gives the worst performance in any Godzilla movie ever. That's right, the worst actor I've ever seen in a Godzilla movie is a *white guy*. Still, it's a solid entry in the Godzilla series, even with Godzooky/Minya/Scrappy-Doo running around the periphery.

Best (subtitled) quote: "Damn that Rodan!"

Godzilla vs. Megaguirus

(2000)

Directed by Masaaki Tezuka

Even if you discount the cartoon where those tools were constantly summoning him via pager and the Marvel comic book where he fought the Avengers (both highly underrated) (fuck you), there are multiple iterations of Godzilla, all divided into various eras/series, some more highly regarded than others. To which I say: *Ha ha ha ha ha ha ha ha ha ha ha ha ha!* **They're all the fucking same.** This entry, for example, is from the *Who Cares?* era, and features Godzilla fighting a giant prehistoric dragonfly, a definite improvement over his usual insect adversary Mothra, who always struck me as a pretty ridiculous foe for Godzilla, King of the Monsters, to have repeatedly lost to. Really, Godzilla, just set something on fire with your nuclear breath and then sit back and watch while she flies into it. Before the big showdown arrives Godzilla battles a swarm of smaller prehistoric dragonflies in a cool pre-game sequence, and Tokyo floods for some reason that wasn't entirely clear (I caught this one on cable TV, and they cut some stuff out so they could run more ads for stupid shit). There are a few limited, crummy cartoon effects (*et tu*, Godzilla?), but, overall, totally recommended. Unless of course you hate Godzilla movies in general, in which case what are you even doing here?

Gorilla at Large

(1954)

Directed by Harmon Jones

You can bet your sweet ass that your hash is pretty much cooked when there's a *Gorilla at Large*.

That's the popular perception, anyway, but you sure wouldn't know it from this movie, which is about *people* killing each other while the gorilla just sort of wanders around, bumping into things. Of course, the first victim *is* discovered inside the gorilla's cage, but even then the authorities aren't so sure the gorilla is responsible. ("All I know is somebody, or something, gave it to him the hard way," says the main cop.) The gorilla's keeper decides to hide the gorilla underwater, in a diving bell, so that it won't be blamed for any subsequent murders, a ridiculously convoluted solution when a good padlock back then only cost what, two or three war bonds? And it doesn't work anyway, because this dumb cop comes bumbling along and accidentally frees the gorilla anyway. (Still, in his defense, who opens a diving bell expecting a gorilla to pop out and make a run for it?) So our movie is halfway over at this point and, finally, the gorilla is legitimately at large.

Now, if you've ever seen a gorilla movie you know that any gorilla-on-the-town's first priority is scaring up a decent piece of ass. True to form, this gorilla goes after the main chick, who has terrific legs and throws her pussy at every guy who looks at her sideways so clearly she's asking for it. (How did we so easily transition from "somewhat promiscuous" to "deserves to be violently raped by a gorilla"? It's complicated. Ask a "men's rights" activist. He'll be able to explain.) Fortunately for her, the gorilla is recaptured before anything ~~arousing~~ disturbing happens, and another cat subsequently confesses to all the murders that occurred previously. It seems that everything's been neatly wrapped up in a nice, tidy little package, but the movie doesn't end so clearly there's a twist coming. Sure enough, the confession was false and the real killer, unlike the gorilla we were promised, remains at large. But then the gorilla escapes again, carrying Legs to the top of a roller coaster, where it's taken out by the cops once and for all. Then Legs is arrested because, apparently, she was the murderer. Frankly, if I was investigating this case I'd give her a pass at this point; she's been humiliated enough. She'd have to blow me though.

You'd think a movie about an unruly gorilla, at large or otherwise, would be full of gorilla-propelled assault and destruction, but this gorilla spends most of his time either hiding or just wandering around. It would have been almost exactly the same movie if it was called, I dunno, "Ostrich at Large" or something. In fact, "Ostrich at Large" sounds a lot more entertaining. Picture an *ostrich* carrying a hot chick up the side up a roller coaster, where it's riddled with bullets before plunging, kicking and squawking, to its death. God damn, that would be hilarious. Not to mention deliciously ironic because, you know, it's a bird, and any other kind of bird could have just flown away. If they'd gone that route, and maybe convinced Legs show off her rack, we might've had a movie here.

Grizzly

(1976)

Directed by William Girdler

This movie may seem out of place in a book about rampaging prehistoric critters, but what's easily missed while enjoying *Grizzly* is that the bear is tentatively identified as *Arctodus ursus horribulis*, a gigantic prehistoric bear that didn't get the memo when all his buddies went extinct approximately one million years ago and has apparently been chilling in this national park ever since, presumably stealing pic-a-nic baskets until something sets him off and he starts killing the fuck out of everybody. (My guess: after one million years as the last of his kind, he *really* needs to get laid.) Regardless of the bear's origins, *Grizzly* is a fucking classic, and if you disagree it's time to cash in your sack because you clearly aren't using it anyway. The premise ("a just-shy-of-actionable ripoff of *Jaws*, on land") is foolproof; it's gory as hell; there are some great/hilarious quotes ("Remember we're probably not looking for a full body."); during the initial search for the bear, a sexy park ranger decides to take a topless shower in a waterfall (you can probably guess how this turns out); the bear pulls down an entire lookout tower and kills the ranger manning it; a small redneck child's leg is graphically torn off; the bear decapitates a goddamned *horse*; they anticipate *Jaws 2* in the scene where the bear cripples a helicopter; and in the end the bear is blown to pieces with a fucking *rocket launcher*. (In the course of **four** *Jaws* movies, not once did anyone think to bring a rocket launcher. Advantage: *Grizzly*.) In short, *Grizzly* fucking rocks. See *Grizzly*.

Bonus:

Grizzly (The Novelization) by Will Collins (1976)

It may seem kind of pointless to "novelize" a movie, but back in the olden days, when there were no online streaming services or double-dip DVD releases or quasi-legal torrent sites, pretty much the only way to "relive" a movie that was no longer playing in theaters was to read the novelization or use your imagination. Unless you wanted to camp out in front of the television and hope that one of the five stations you got (six, if you counted that fuzzy one from Chicago) decided to show it someday. Seriously, kids, the 20th century was tough. You need to count your fucking blessings.

Besides being your only option, old novelizations did have one other thing going for them: sometimes they contained throwaway lines or even entire scenes that didn't end up in the final version of the movie, some of which have since been lost forever. Like it's a little-known fact, but in the first cut of *The Empire Strikes Back* Princess Leia blows just about everybody. Don't believe me? Well fuck you. Anyway, in the *Grizzly* novelization, we actually learn *why* our titular (heh) grizzly is suddenly so ill-tempered: it has a toothache. I'm totally serious. There's also an exclusive-to-the-book sex scene between the main guy and his girl (which wasn't missed; the actress they cast as the girlfriend was pretty rogue), and an additional bit at the end where the main guy flips his shit and starts wildly chucking hand grenades at the bear from a helicopter. This last bit is so awesome/hilarious, in fact, that I'll ignore the part where this same guy uses the order the bear's victims were killed in to make an important point, but has the order completely wrong. The only other misstep is the inclusion of a handful of new characters who appear, do nothing of import, and then vanish, never to be referred to again. My guess is that the writer had every intention of padding out the story – and inflating the body count – by killing these assholes off, but then he got distracted and/or drunk and just plain forgot he put them in there. That's pretty bush league, but then I guess you can't expect *too* much from the fucking novelization of *Grizzly*.

Grizzly 2 (Workprint)

(1985)

Directed by André Szöts

First off, to the guy in Orlando who told me that I was an idiot because this movie didn't exist: Eat it. Eat it with two sides of your choice, asshole.

Grizzly 2, which totally exists, was shot in the 1980s, but due to some legal hullabaloo it was never quite finished and has been a persistent urban legend ever since, at least among people who spend any amount of time thinking about things like *Grizzly 2*. At one point it was bundled with some assets seized by the FDIC, at which point I actually tried to buy it from them only to miss my window of opportunity by *that* much. For real, I came *so fucking close* to **owning** *Grizzly 2*. You better believe I would've released it too, unlike every other prick who's ended up with it. Fortunately, someone finally got fed up, stole it, and put it on the Internet. After all the work I put in tracking this fucking movie down as it changed hands over the years I was kinda pissed that several other movie-nerd bitches beat me to the reviewing punch, but hey, at least we all get to see it now. In your fucking face, copyright holders of *Grizzly 2*.

The story's pretty straightforward: someone kills Brother Bear, so Mama Bear goes on a rampage that ends backstage at this huge outdoor ~~rock pop~~ gay pride concert. And when I say "huge" I'm talking Woodstock huge, with multiple semis required to truck in all the gear and equipment. And hey, to judge from the distinctive paint job on one of these semis, the services of a Mr. B.J. McKay were among the many secured for this task. (And his best friend Bear! I get it!) Naturally this whole setup is just an excuse to eat up lots of screen time with endless scenes of band members practicing, playing, and, for some reason, working out, but I didn't find this material particularly intolerable. Besides, I kinda liked the song that goes "Don't stop to take a shit / don't stop to lose your grip..." When you won't slow down for pooping *or* insanity, you're definitely hard core. Of course there's plenty of disposable, time-killing drama too, mainly involving the park ranger's daughter and her crush on one of the singers, but weirdly enough this movie's biggest emotional scene is between two of the (human) bad guys. Seriously, I thought these fags were gonna kiss. I'm glad they worked everything out before they died horribly though.

Gore-wise, there's not much to see, just a couple of impalings and some aftermath stuff. There's no tits either, but there are plenty of hotties wandering around, the standout being the concert producer's blonde assistant. (Watch carefully when she bumps into the two cats at the very beginning - I think one of them cops a feel.) As for the grizzly, we don't see much of it at all. When Mama Bear is the focus of a scene it's generally shot from her POV, but with the camera placed so high that we have no choice but to assume that she has the power of flight. Or maybe she just walks around on her hind legs a lot. Aw, she thinks she's people! We do see the bitch at the very end though and I have to say, she looks pretty damned cool. And I'm happy to report that she does get to tip over a forklift before the humans finally finish her off, resulting in the single most hilarious shot in bear movie history. The thrilling climax is incomplete and a bit hard to follow, but apparently the bear is ultimately electrocuted to death. I suppose it makes perfect sense that *Grizzly 2* would unabashedly rip off *Jaws 2*. Why fuck with a successful formula?

Believe it or not there are a lot of famous people in this movie, including Indiana Jones' Egyptian friend Sallah, George Clooney, and even Charlie Sheen, not winning as he's butchered by a cheesed-off prehistoric bear. But hey, that's what he gets for hiking into an area that's clearly marked "Closed Because Of Bear Danger". My favorite line, meanwhile, comes courtesy the main chick after someone shoots the wrong grizzly: "The man's colorblind! He can't even tell what a male looks like!" What?

Unquestionably flawed but thoroughly entertaining, there's no reason this flick can't be polished up and finally fostered on an indifferent, baffled public. Just pimp-slap the climax into shape, have some computer nerd whip up a cartoon bear to insert where necessary, call in a favor over at Netflix, and be done with it. The end result couldn't possibly be any worse than your standard Syphilis Channel movie.

Head

(1968)

Directed by Bob Rafelson

The Monkees were conceived as an even-worse Beatles (thanks, dickheads), but to their credit they manged to pull themselves up by their bootblacks and recorded several good songs. One of them ("I'm Not Your Stepping Stone") even became a punk standard, which is more than you can say for John Lennon and company. (Seriously, "I Am the Walrus"? Fuck off.) But when the Monkees' tired-ass shtick had run its course (this didn't take long) and their silly television show got canceled they just couldn't let it go, so they decided to "reinvent" themselves as a grown-up band. Their first step was to star in a freaky-deaky, psychedelic movie, one that all the kids could grok to while on acid, man. Unfortunately, their approach to psychedelia was like Miley Cyrus's approach to trashy sex appeal: artlessly curb-stomping you with it while clearly having only the vaguest idea of what it actually is. Except of course Miley Cyrus can pull her tongue back into her mouth and she's still one of the hottest women on the planet. There was no way the Monkees were getting *Head* back into their collective mouths. See, even the most whacked-out stream-of-consciousness horseshit needs to have some identifiable, unifying theme to make it relatable ("sucking ass" doesn't count), and *Head* is just too impenetrable. To the casual observer who didn't dream up the script while smoking weed and then write it while on acid (seriously, that's how it supposedly went down) it's just a bunch of dumb, random crap. I didn't mind their pre-fab records or their pre-fab television show at all, but if this is what the Monkees were "really" about then I'm sorry, but they can suck my dick.

Hitler's Jurassic Zoo

(2014)

Produced by Quickfire Media

Okay, I know I said I was staying away from documentaries, but who could resist this description, via my hyperbolic (and confrontationally incompetent) cable company:

The Nazis conduct experiments to bring extinct animals back to life, with the hopes of releasing the creatures into hunting parks...

Ha ha ha ha ha ha ha! As anyone with basic cable knows, retard-umentaries credit the Nazis with everything from time travel to inventing UFOs to being first on the moon (I kid you not, I taped three different documentaries, making these exact three claims, off three different channels, on the very same day), but if you go into this expecting some equally deranged twaddle, like maybe cloned allosaurs running down Nazi luminaries in the aftermath a big game hunt gone wrong, you'll be just as disappointed as we were. ("Maybe they'll work in a ghost story too," suggested Brittany, my teenage ward, as the show started.) Naturally, what really happened was a lot more prosaic: in 1941 the Nazis set aside a game preserve (okay, so this did require displacing and/or killing 20,000 or so people, but what did you expect? They're Nazis.) and then bred the biggest cows possible to stock the place with. So basically their scheme had more in common with McDonald's than Jurassic Park. But let's face it, no one would have watched this show if it was called "Hitler's Cows". Unless maybe it was a documentary about morbidly obese skinhead chicks. Although even that is a pretty niche fetish. I hope.

Horror Express

(1972)

Directed by Gene Martin

This scientist unearths a frozen caveman, buys it a ticket (I guess) and takes it on the train home with him. What he doesn't know is that the caveman is possessed by an alien, and en route it pops to life and starts killing people. As with most problems shooting it seems like the best available option, but when they do the intangible alien just flees the caveman's body and possesses someone else. This crazy priest, meanwhile, is convinced that the alien is the Devil, and I guess he got all F's in priest school because he decides to throw in with it. Up to this point *Horror Express* is a pretty solid movie, but then TV's Kojak shows up, sporting a faggoty fur coat, spouting all sorts of melodramatic nonsense, and just generally being an intolerable jackass. (Seriously, if ever you want to throw an anchor around your movie that will drag it all the way down to an ocean floor made entirely of shit, just cast fucking Kojak. He could single-handedly torpedo a Oscar-nominated documentary about nudity starring Megan Fox, Katy Perry, and the girl you had a crush on in tenth grade.) The alien doesn't have any patience for Kojak's crap either, so it ices him immediately, then resurrects all the people it killed as zombies. Cavemen, aliens, and now zombies? Enough is clearly enough, so the authorities reroute the train to a set of tracks that will take it right off a cliff. I'm not sure why anyone would even lay train tracks that lead off a cliff, but they sure come in handy this time and that's the end of *that* fucking alien. It takes balls to cram this many ~~desperate~~ disparate elements into a single movie, but I have to admit, it all works. Except for Kojak. He's a goddamned idiot.

Ice Age 3: Dawn of the Dinosaurs

(2009)

Directed by Carlos Saldanha

I've mentioned my preference for prehistoric mammals over dinosaurs, but even I'm forced to admit that the biggest ones – like the giant sloth – were "gentle giants", more likely to kill you by accident rather than by intentional, horror-movie design. As for the smaller ones, well, a lot of them look like something you could pick up down at that shady pet store that only sells exotics you never even heard of and are forced to look up in your box of Safari Cards™ before you remember that the Internet exists. (Incidentally, why is there no secondary collectors' market for Safari Cards? Given the ubiquitous ads for them in the 1970s you'd think *some* idiot would still be trying to collect them all.) In short, most prehistoric mammals were *cute*, perfectly suited for a family-friendly, merchandise-friendly, me-unfriendly cartoon. Too bad the best anyone could come up with was 2002's *Ice Age*, a million years in the making and instantly a legendary piece of shit. The characters were unlikable and annoying, the jokes were lazy and uninspired, and the top-billed voice was none other than recognized fuckhole Ray Romano, star of the reprehensible, erroneously-titled sitcom *Everybody Loves Raymond*. Nevertheless, *Ice Age 2* came out a few years later, followed by this one, which features baby dinosaurs as well, adding an unwelcome *Land Before Time CXXXVIII* vibe to the already pungent mix. Eat my chariot-driven fuck, *Ice Age*.

Obviously I approached this flick with malice and forespite, which it totally deserves given its dumb sitcom setup (way to exploit your unique characters and setting, asshats) and for continuing to provide human tapeworm Ray Romano with gainful employment. That said, it's surprisingly easy to forget that ~~Everybody Loves~~ Raymond is involved when you can't see his dopey, rage-inducing face, and to be honest there are a few semi-clever set pieces, not to mention some unexpected instances of animals dying horribly, cooked alive in lava and whatnot. Too bad the sloth isn't among them. Of course the song "Walk the Dinosaur" makes an appearance (the habits of a bottom-feeding hack are so predictable), and, for the kids, there's a castration joke. Oh, there's a gay joke too, but if you're the type of parent who doesn't want you kids knowing about the gays then you're probably one of those people who insists that dinosaur fossils were planted in the ground by the Devil to trick us, and you wouldn't be watching this movie anyway.

Iceman

(1984)

Directed by Fred Schepisi

In my review for *Baby: Secret of the Lost Legend* (it was just a few pages ago; if you can't remember that far back, you smoke entirely too much weed) I noted the 1980s' penchant for movies about the appearance of an unusual being and the ensuing debate regarding how quickly and painfully it should be dissected until a small child, a pretty girl, or a liberal renders the matter moot by helping it escape. In this case the unusual being is a caveman, frozen in ice, who at some point in the narrative may or may nor have been dubbed the "Iceman", not to be confused with the character of the same name who appears in the gay-pride classic *Top Gun* (1986), or the X-Man Iceman, also recently revealed to be gay. Not that I blame the latter for giving up on chicks, seeing as, in his first miniseries (also 1984), the girl he dug blew him off *so she could knock boots with her own dad*. That would turn anybody queer.

So anyway, the scientists who discover caveman Iceman are shocked to learn that he's still alive, and not at all possessed by an alien. (Points off.) Flush with scientific dickbaggery, they decide to place Iceman in a tiny, artificial forest environment, I guess so they can study his reaction to what, from his perspective, can only be described as "incomprehensible horror-magic insanity". Somehow though it never dawns on anyone involved that Iceman might get bored, walk more than 20 feet in any one direction, and escape. Of course that's exactly what happens, and in an exciting movie the next thing to occur would be a violent caveman rampage, complete with cheerleader rape, which is a perfectly acceptable monster movie trope because look what she's wearing. Unfortunately, this movie thinks it's important or something, so instead Iceman is re-apprehended and we're forced to sit through scene after scene of the main guy trying to befriend him, and, eventually, assisting him in escape attempt #2. This second escape attempt gets Iceman killed, evoking a huge smile from the main guy because... he's an asshole, I guess? Seriously, if this is really our main guy's idea of "helping" I move that we introduce him to Mac (of *...and Me*) and Harry (of *...and the Hendersons*) immediately.

Ice Road Terror

(2011)

Directed by Terry Ingram

You know, it actively pisses me off that a show as mind-numbingly one-note as *Ice Road Truckers* could run for (as of this writing) *nine seasons*, not including spin-offs. Spin-offs! How many miles can these dickhats drive with nothing really happening before it's no longer engaging television? I'll give you a hint: it's a number less than zero. Obviously nothing is ever too stupid or pointless to become successful, and in 2011 *Ice Road Truckers* was popular enough with people aged 18-34 who don't get out of the house much that the Syphilis Channel decided to make a movie ripping it off, or what their lawyers would doubtlessly call an "homage". Of course we are talking about the Syphilis Channel here, so this movie features a prehistoric cartoon monster trying to eat the truckers, but as ridiculous as this is at least it's slightly more interesting than watching Earl slide into yet another ditch. (If there isn't a guy named "Earl" on *Ice Road Truckers*, I think we can all agree that there should be.) Of course *Ice Road Terror* is relentlessly dumb, and it's full of insultingly contrived, action-citment feats of daring-duh that make no sense whatsoever and/or are completely unnecessary. (Then again, why put all that wear and tear on your brakes when you can simply leap from one moving truck to another?) Oh well, at least it's gory, and the main chick is reasonably cute if you can ignore that big thing on her nose, which isn't *too* difficult given the size of her tits. Don't get me wrong, I wouldn't watch this movie if there was anything better on, but let's face it, there usually isn't.

In the Shadow of Kilimanjaro

(1986)

Directed by Raju Patel

Dateline: Africa. Due to a particularly brutal drought (also known as "living in Africa") starving baboons are on the rampage, and monkeys are the last animal you want gunning for you given their ability to open doors, use simple tools, ride unicycles, smoke cigars, etc. Also, I feel compelled to point out that this situation represents an abject failure on the part of USA for Africa, a failure compounded by their terrible fucking album, which actually complicated the world hunger issue by making everyone who listened to it puke. (I swear, if killer monkeys had overrun the recording studio and wiped out all 44 members of USA for Africa, the only ones we would've mourned would be Willie Nelson and Cyndi Lauper's legs.) (Seriously, universe, why couldn't this have happened?) Eventually our main cast is forced to barricade themselves inside the local hotel while endless waves of ~~zombies~~ baboons try to break in and eat them, only to be saved at the last minute when it *finally* rains. Because hunger-crazed baboons can eat rain, I guess? The scene where a baboon stows away on an airplane and causes it to crash, while hilarious, is a bit much for a movie that's overtly striving to be realistic ("It's a *true story* about a *savage terror* that *really happened.*"), but there is some decent gore, the image of dozens of baboons bum-rushing hapless schmucks is pretty effective, and there are numerous instances of monkeys falling out of trees after being shot, which never failed to crack me up. Too bad none of them were smoking cigars at the time. *That* would be fucking classic.

La isla de los dinosaurios

(1967)

Directed by Rafael Portillo

¿Dinosaurios? *¡Ay, caramba!* Mexicans crash-land on Dinosaur Island, the dinosaurs take the opportunity to sample some Mexican cuisine, and my deck never gets built. Ha ha! This flick is only available in Mexican because it's not good enough to even bother translating it into English (to put this into perspective, most Jesús Franco movies have been translated into English), but rest assured, you aren't missing much: the dinosaur scenes are mostly stolen from other movies, and the bulk of the plot concerns a lovesick caveman who abducts one of the main chicks and, eventually, introduces her to his mom. (Naturally, mom hates her.) The two main chicks take several ill-advised swims; there's a long scene where two cavemen fight while several cavewomen look on, clearly unimpressed; and caveman sign language for "Are you hungry?" could easily be misinterpreted as "May I fist you?" Seriously, Mexico, movies aren't for you. Stick to tacos and Glori Trevi. Those are your strengths.

"I Was Afraid to Love You"

(1985)

(Love Theme from *Godzilla 1985*)

In 1984, after a nine year hiatus, they decided to start making Godzilla movies again, and the first new one was released in the U.S. as *Godzilla 1985* because that title wouldn't sound dated at all in just a few months. Dr Pepper quickly jumped on board, not-so-subtly inserting their product into the American version (I swear, people must walk past like fifty Dr Pepper machines in the course of this movie) and whipping up some Dr Pepper commercials wherein Godzilla and a second giant monster enjoy the refreshing taste of Dr Pepper while the Japanese cheer him on ("Diet Dr Pepper! Diet Dr Pepper!"). By far the best thing to come out of this heavy-handed union though was the preposterous music video for "I Was Afraid to Love You", a low-key pop song that doesn't even appear in the movie, sung by a chick who is never identified, featuring images of Godzilla destroying shit, Godzilla quaffing Dr Pepper, people standing suspiciously close to Dr Pepper logos, and wholly random images like a small child playing with a robot dinosaur. It's so jaw-droppingly shameless that even MTV – who in 1985 ran almost nothing but music videos 24 hours a day and thus had a shitload of time to fill – allegedly aired it only twice, and one of those times was at the insistence of Elvira during her 1986 Halloween special, because nobody says no to Elvira. *Godzilla 1985* is a pretty good flick, but I would never buy it on DVD unless they released some sort of super-special edition featuring both cuts of the movie (Japanese and American), the Dr Pepper commercials, *and* this awful/brilliant music video. Are you listening, Criterion Collection? Stop dicking around with all that Merchant Ivory art-house bullshit and give the people what we want.

Journey to the Center of the Earth

(1959)

Directed by Henry Levin

One good thing about old movies is that you don't have to deal with a bunch of shitty, fake-looking cartoon effects. This one, for example, uses "rear-projection", which is when you physically place the actor in front of something you filmed previously, usually something that it would be difficult to obtain or create, or for the actor to interact with, in real life. Take an early shot in this movie, for example, where they use rear-projection to show the main guy standing in front of... er, a shelf of books? Okay, fine, sometimes the people who made these old movies were just stupendously lazy.

This flick also makes use of another old-school special effects process, popularly known as "suck it, PETA". This is when you take a regular, everyday animal and glue stuff all over it until it looks like an approximation of a prehistoric monster or at the very least a lizard with crap glued all over it. This movie represents the pinnacle of this process, because the lizards in *JttCotE '59* really do make for passable Dimetrodons, prehistoric reptiles that all the documentaries are careful to stress weren't, technically, dinosaurs, but fuck you, documentaries, they were totally dinosaurs. To say these special effects were groundbreaking for the time would be an irresponsible lie (cf. the original *King Kong*, made decades previously), but other than that this movie looks really good, featuring cool-ass cavern sets filled with crystals, or salt, or giant mushrooms. Speaking of looking good, the fiancée one guy leaves behind is a *no-holds-barred sexpot knockout*. I'm sorry, Science, but if I had access to that the only center I'd be journeying to would be the center of her pussy. Too bad she's only in a few scenes, most of which involve pining and none of which involve her lathering up her breasts. In her biggest scene she "comically" falls down a ladder and we're not even treated to a solid upskirt shot. More unwelcome "comedy" is provided by a pet duck that's inexplicably along for the ride, although to be fair the first scene with the duck is legitimately funny so its presence is only mostly annoying. Other pluses include a wholly unexpected explosion (spoiler warning); the part where our crew actually reaches the literal center of the Earth (it mugs them); the discovery of Atlantis; a hilarious POV shot from inside a giant Gila monster's mouth; and the fact that, during their final escape through the volcano, the main chick is clearly having an orgasm. Too bad the first half hour focuses almost entirely on our heroes' race with a shady rival to see who can get to the *entrance* to the center of the Earth first, a conflict rendered suddenly, unsatisfactorily moot when the rival is unexpectedly found dead in his hotel room. Are you fucking kidding me? Thanks for wasting everyone's time, movie.

Journey to the Center of the Earth

(1967)

Produced by Filmation

The 1959 version of *JttCotE* was so successful (I hate to admit this, but it was probably because of the duck) that this eight-years-later Saturday morning cartoon take was actually based on it instead of the original book, going so far as to resurrect the duck and the main bad guy, both of whom died in the movie. (Yes, the 1959 movie actually had the balls to kill off the comedic-relief duck, another point in its favor.) Of course there are plenty of dinosaurs and cavemen on hand, but most episodes are a nonsensical orgy of random monster attacks, kind of like a Dungeons & Dragons adventure written by an eleven-year-old who owns *all* the books and supplements, even the inexcusably stupid ones (*Dungeons & Dragons Set 5: Immortals Rules*). In one episode alone our heroes might encounter a dinosaur, a yellow bigfoot, a fairy tale giant, and a gigantic pill bug, plus several more. The human villains, meanwhile, repeatedly attempt to foil the good guys via covered pits, which works often enough that the good guys should really be embarrassed. Not to mention the writers. Plotless and totally ridiculous, it's pretty much an endurance test, despite the occasional appearance of some cool, little-seen prehistoric monsters. The good guys surf a lava flow. ("Wheee!") There's "boiling quicksand". (Seriously, it's not enough that it's quicksand, or that it's boiling, it has to be both?) "I only hope the rope will hold our weight!" says the main guy, right before they use the rope in question to cross the boiling quicksand *two at a time*. You goddamned idiots.

Hard to believe this is the same company that, the following decade, produced truly brilliant cartoons like *Flash Gordon*, *Fat Albert*, and *Tarzan, Lord of the Jungle*. Of course, later still they developed the gay pride version of He-Man where he subdued male enemies by dry-humping them from behind, so I guess it's not *that* hard to believe.

A Journey to the Center of the Earth

(1977)

Directed by Richard Slapczynski

Local TV stations used to trot this cartoon out on holiday afternoons (when no one else was watching TV anyway), often under the guise of it being "educational" (because it was based on a book). So while dad was screaming at mom for burning the turkey and older sister was making out with a cousin behind the garage ("It's not incest because we won't get caught!") younger kids lucky enough to stumble upon it could thrill to an animated adventure full of bad science, irresponsible property destruction, mysterious disappearances and deaths, giant bugs, psychedelic light shows, prehistoric mammals, and, of course, dinosaurs. Like most *JttCotE* adaptations, the story's more than half over by the time these clowns actually reach the center of the Earth, and more time is wasted on a tiresome sideplot concerning two of the main professor's rivals, but overall it's a pretty solid adaptation, way less insulting to the source material than the many live-actor versions that have appeared over the years, with their tacked-on ducks and has-been sitcom stars and Brendan Frasers. Hell, it even retains the opening article in the title. Is it better than making out with your cousin? Probably not, but in those pre-cable, pre-Internet days, goofy, mysterious cartoons like this one (Who made it? Why?) were like a gift from the gods, and became schoolyard legends among the few who saw them, especially if they were never aired a second time, which was often the case with fickle, dickhead local TV stations. Would you believe that the local NBC affiliate in Toledo, Ohio actually refused to air *Halloween* (1978) when it made its network television premiere in 1981? For Christ's sake, it was an *edited-for-TV version*. How fucking pussified and repressive can you get?

Journey to the Center of the Earth

(1999)

Directed by George Miller

To judge from the embarrassing results, *A Journey to the Center of the Earth* is a difficult story to film, but this version starts out okay, featuring some clever dialogue and admirably grey-area morals on the part of our heroes, who actually become arms smugglers to facilitate their journey to (the entrance to) the center of the Earth. Why go to all this trouble in the first place? To track down the main chick's husband, who disappeared down the Earth's butthole while hunting for gold. Not because he needed the money, mind you, but solely to trump his wife and *her* family money. I'll bet his penis is really small too. Speaking of, when they finally find the guy he's ruling over a primitive tribe that is just sick with hot-ass chicks, especially the redhead who falls for one of our main guys, who is so achingly fine that I'm not even gonna question where she buys her lip gloss or gets her hair done. Maybe at the Salon at the Center of the Earth. Oh, there's a second tribe as well, and the two tribes are essentially at war over the most valuable resource the inner world has to offer: a mysterious strain of super marijuana! I'm pretty sure that wasn't in the original story, but it's fucking awesome and hilarious and a welcome inclusion. The cartoon effects are fucking terrible, some of the worst, and sometimes the music is entirely inappropriate (all funny and dopey when something suspenseful or exciting is going on, for example), but the story moves at a fair clip, the chicks are incredible, and the lizard men who show up to complicate matters are pretty cool, so until they produce an all-nudie adaptation starring any combination of Kimber Riddle, Kesha Sebert, Avril Lavigne, Juliet Landau, Ellie Kemper, or Miley Cyrus, this is definitely the version to see.

P.S. Also Kirsten Dunst.

Journey to the Center of the Earth

(2008)

Directed by Eric Brevig

If there's one thing every iteration of *JttCotE* is good at, it's dicking around for half the running time (or more) before anyone even *sees* the goddamned center of the Earth. Seriously, dilwads, this story doesn't need to play out in real time. Okay, fine, so the original book essentially did the same thing (the title IS ***Journey to** the Center of the Earth*, not *Shit We Did at the Center of the Earth*), but isn't that why one makes a movie out of a book in the first place? To improve on the source material by changing shit around, speeding up the pacing, and, ideally, adding some tits? So kudos to this take for actually updating the story to modern times and mixing things up a little bit. In this version the original book is basically a true story, and when terminal dimwit Brendan Fraser (*Encino Man* is apparently a true story in this universe too) figures this out, he makes the criminally irresponsible decision to drag his 13-year-old asswipe of a nephew along with him on a *Journey... to the Center...* blah blah, you know. The mine car sequence is kinda dumb (and far too reminiscent of *Indiana Jones and the Temple of Doom*), they impart entirely too many facts about geology (stop tricking me into learning shit, movie; that's the exact opposite of what Hollywood is supposed to stand for), and there are several distracting instances of people thrusting shit directly at the camera (this came out smack-dab in the middle of the third, longest, and most painful fad for 3-D movies), but overall there's more good than bad here and in the end it's a fair adventure movie, albeit one that would have benefited considerably from a larger main cast. You can never have to many superfluous redshirts on hand to gorily kill off via dinosaur. Also, seeing as they added the business about the underground world rapidly growing hotter and hotter – to the point where our crew has to return to the surface as quickly as possible, or be cooked alive – wouldn't it make sense, sooner or later, for the main chick to take her shirt off? Seriously, I'm just being practical here.

Journey to the Center of the Earth

(2008)

Directed by T.J. Scott

As you can see, the book *Journey to the Center of the Earth* is a perennial favorite with moviemakers, because it's a timeless classic with wide appeal and, far more importantly, it's firmly in the public domain. This one was undoubtedly counting on the big-screen Brendan Fraser *JttCotE*, released the same year, to be a hit, at which point they would clean up by coasting on its scraps. That was their last good idea, because from there they cast the kid from *Silver Spoons* (1982-1987) as the main guy and then decided that, when we finally get to the center of the Earth, the big payoff would be a single cartoon dinosaur and a bunch of Eskimos.

I can't remember the last time I was so disappointed when I got to the center of something.

Journey to the Center of Time

(1967)

Directed by David L. Hewitt

Oh my god, I was so sick of *Journey to the Center of the Earth* by this point. (A piece of advice: if you ever decide to watch a bunch of movies with a similar theme, never insist on watching them in alphabetical order.) Which is why I'm glad that *this* journey is to the gooey, nougaty center of time, where progress runs backwards and it's perfectly legal to hook up with a thirteen-year-old girl. Also known as the Republic of Niger.

So, these scientists are experimenting with time travel, but in a grounded, nontheatrical manner that in no way involves nuclear-powered DeLoreans or Jane Wiedlin as Joan of Arc (so fucking fine). This means that for their research to have any practical, real-world value they need results, dammit, and the guy funding this temporal bake sale isn't seeing enough of those to keep coughing up the dough. ("Dough", "bake sale"... see what I did there?) Well, brainiacs who are about to get their funding pulled tend to take chances, so they agree on a conservative test run: just a short jaunt around the clock, maybe 24 hours or so. Knobs are twisted, brows furrow, the music swells, and suddenly the whole lab has been transported 5000 years into the future! Oops! So what is it like 5000 years in the future? Some aliens led by Wonder Woman's boyfriend (AKA the most ineffectual man ever) quickly fill the scientists in: Earth is a nuclear wasteland, and future humans are such unapologetic dicks that they immediately started a war with the arriving aliens, whose only crime was picking the wrong planet on which to make their interstellar pit stop. Sounds exciting, right? Wrong. Mostly it's just people talking, often while standing next to one or maybe two props in a black, featureless void. Seriously, it's like a Samuel Beckett play or something. Fleeing this minimalist idiocy, the scientists over-compensate again and, finally, end up in dinosaur times, where we briefly glimpse dinosaurs lifted from other, equally crappy movies and one dolt falls into the hot lava. When they miss their chrono-target a second time and end up a day early, we're treated to a minisode version of everything we just saw before our surviving idiots are lost in time forever, and good riddance to the lot of them. Although to be fair, I would bang the chick. Maybe blow a load in that absurd, piled-up hair of hers. It'd be the end of time before she got that mess cleaned out, that's for sure.

Jug Man

(2003)

Directed by Scott Heming

If you asked every single human being on Earth what the world needs you'd get a lot of crazy, highly-specific answers, but I'll bet not one of them would say "A wholly-acknowledged parody of a shitty, decade-old Pauly Shore movie starring the Archie Comics gang." They say we get what we deserve, not what we need, though, so in this cartoon movie the city's new geothermal heating system thaws out a caveman who bears a striking resemblance to resident moron Jughead and eats everything in sight, including cockroaches and a dead tapeworm. And that's probably the *least* weird thing happening in Archie's hometown of Riverdale, which seems to possess an unusually high level of technology: there's a fully-automated drive-thru restaurant; resident nerd Denton owns a functioning Star Trek-style tricorder and a universal language translator; and token asshole Reggie has access to several fully-autonomous, moonwalking robots that wear sunglasses and, in a rational world, would be rapping about the dangers of drugs in a 1980s' PSA. In addition, bears roam the streets unmolested, and, if I'm understanding correctly, at least some forms of slavery are still legal within the city limits.

Clearly the world of Archie bears no resemblance to our current reality, but if you can get past that (drugs will help) this movie is passably funny on occasion, and at one point there's a pretty cool scene where a woolly mammoth takes on a garbage truck. (This mammoth later attends homecoming.) *Jug Man* doesn't so much end as aimlessly ramble its way to a non-conclusion, but there is a funny twist in the final moments, and even when depicted via middling animation Veronica Lodge remains one of the hottest comic book chicks of all time.

Okay, *Jug Man*. I suppose your existence is justified.

Jurassic Attack

(2013)

Directed by Anthony Fankhauser

After the world's most poorly-edited plane crash, two zipheads are attacked by a dinosaur, firmly establishing that this dinosaur movie is, in fact, about dinosaurs. Arriving in the same general vicinity five years later: a party of gung-ho military asswipes, under orders from Parker Lewis to rescue this hot, underwear-clad ~~model~~ biochemist from terrorists. Stumbling through the jungle with all the skill of a troop of drunken Boy Scouts, they're quickly attacked by dinosaurs too. Seems there's a whole valley full of the critters that Google Earth somehow missed, and the people in this movie keep waltzing right into it. Years ago, awful, generic, crap movies like this one would serve solely as video store filler (you can only stock so many copies of *Star Trek IV*); now they basically serve the same purpose on Netflix. The effects are bad, the plot is non-existent, and the acting is fucking *terrible,* even for an auto-fail, tax-write-off project like this. It's all so lazy and slight I doubt there was even a script. The director probably pointed the camera at the cast, said "Dinosaurs!", and just let them make it up as they went along, keeping every single take no matter how nonsensical their dialogue turned out to be. How else do you explain exchanges like this:

CHICK: "There's something amazing about this place. With enough funding and the right equipment, [incomprehensible] could learn!"

SOLDIER #1: "You gotta be kidding me!"

CHICK: "This place has an incredible evolutionary advantage! And, it's as if it traveled back in time."

SOLDIER #1: "What!?"

SOLDIER #2: "It's a metaphor."

SOLDIER #3: "It's definitely not a metaphor!"

That's not writing, that's four people trying to hold a lofty conversation when at least two of them are hopelessly stoned. In the end, the survivors are spirited off in a helicopter, and once they're safely away the main guy turns around and blows up one final T. rex with a rocket launcher, for absolutely no reason whatsoever. Worldview-altering biological discovery? Unprecedented scientific value? Endangered species? Whatever, you tree-hugging hippies.

Jurassic Hunters

(2015)

Directed by Ari Novak

This "dinosaurs vs. modern-day cowboys" (i.e. not really cowboys) (sorry, modern-day cowboys, but it's true) movie started life as "Jurassic Hunters" (to cash in on the public's fondness for *Jurassic Park*), was re-titled "Cowboys vs. Dinosaurs" (to cash in on the public's ~~fondness~~ vague recollection of *Cowboys & Aliens*), and then because "Jurassic Hunters" again once *Jurassic World* went into production. Clearly it's a labor of love and not 90 minutes of cynically-produced-and-marketed sewer-drippings at all. The cynical drippings begin when the Lando Mining Company (oh, fuck off), while digging for unobtainium, unwittingly dredges up a whole mess of dinosaurs that immediately start preying on the area's sizable population of mediocre, underwear-clad chicks. Oh, and sometimes these dinosaurs explode when shot, because this awful movie wasn't stupid enough already. Crummy effects, laughable gore, dumb story, terrible acting, and our main guy is a charisma-free dickbag who was either severely constipated throughout the entire production or just looks that way all the time, in which case, seriously, don't cast that guy. On top of all that, there are at least a couple of scenes that really needed to be re-shot or re-recorded or fixed in post or some damn thing, like the part where the sheriff sagely informs his girl that "There's no sense in reliving the **path**." Overall it's a pretty wretched experience, and how much you get out of it will depend almost entirely on how much you enjoy seeing mediocre chicks in their underwear. I consider myself a more-than-casual fan, but there's only so much dumb a person can take and in the end the only thing that got me through this depressing turd was a single legitimately talented (and uncommonly fine) actress who will forever be remembered by me as "the chick who escapes by hiding inside a dryer at the laundromat". Oh, she's one of the main characters, but even with the help of the Internet I haven't been able figure out what her character's *name* is. Seriously, that's how slipshod this movie is.

Jurassic Park III

(2001)

Directed by Joe Johnston

"How can you write a book about dinosaur movies and not review *Jurassic Park*?" Fuck you, that's how. I'm not wasting any more of my time on *Jurassic* epic disappointment *Park* because it Jurassic sucks. Sure, the first appearance of the T. rex is acceptably badass, and I like the part where the truck chases those people down the tree. That was inventive. The bulk of *Jurassic Park* is trite, corny, puke bait though, loaded with stock characters, obnoxious children, and cloying, family-friendly horseshit. I actually thought Part 2 was infinitely better: it has better characters, better set-pieces, more dinosaur attacks, and my drastically lowered expectations probably didn't hurt. Well, here's Part 3 and Part 3 in a series is usually when diminishing returns grinds that gravy train to a halt, prompting the producers to start peddling the usual BS about how "it was always conceived as a trilogy". This time we've got yet another child lost in Jurassic Park (along with his, *ahem,* adult male "companion"), prompting his parents and their redshirt dino-bait entourage to come looking for him. The child in question is hella annoying – to the point where this movie would be infinitely more satisfying if, ultimately, all his parents ever found was his skeleton – but his mom is hotness personified, so I guess one negates the other, putting us right back at zero. Of course, no one watches a *Jurassic Park* movie for the kid, or even tits; they're here for the dinosaur attacks and there are plenty of those. And while the dinosaurs are mostly cartoons, even decades later *Jurassic Park* is one of the only movies to ever feature decent cartoon effects (sad, isn't it?) – and the sequels have continued that tradition – so if nothing else at least they look pretty good. The whole "raptors were/are smart enough to set traps and possibly compose moving, ground-breaking sonnets" angle is fucking retarded though, and so is the *Peter Pan* lift wherein a dinosaur swallows the dad's cell phone, which proceeds to ring constantly, repeatedly alerting everyone to said dinosaur's presence. Are you fucking kidding me? Who keeps calling that goddamn phone anyway? Did this guy not let people know that he would be unavailable because he was going to look for his son on Dinosaur Island?

Jurassic World

(2015)

Directed by Colin Trevorrow

"Star Lord vs. dinosaurs" sounds like it would be the cover blurb for a 1970s' Marvel comic book, one of the magazine-sized black & white ones that occasionally had tits in them. But, nope, it's basically the plot of *Jurassic World*, the fourth, and only second or third dumbest, entry in the *Jurassic Park* franchise. The premise is that, despite the oodles of people who were killed the first time, ~~Westworld~~ Jurassic World (née Jurassic Park) has been re-opened to the public. This time however, having learned from their mistakes (Ha ha! *Of course* I'm kidding.), they've DNAed up a new, mutant dinosaur that's bigger and hungrier than anything that ever actually existed and turns out to be smart enough to out-think at least the secondary characters. The dinosaurs look great, as always, and LOTS of people are killed, even if considerations like being able to license tie-in Lego sets did preclude them from delivering on any real gore. (Still, the limey chick's demise, at least, was pretty horrific for a "dry" death.) And for all the shit it ate online in the weeks leading up to the release, the scene where the mosasaur eats the great white shark is pretty damned cool. There are some nice, little touches too, like the disagreement about the original Jurassic Park t-shirt, rampaging dinosaurs referred to as a "containment anomaly", and the Imax gag. You'll have to watch *very* carefully to catch my favorite bit though: the guy who makes a point of saving not one but *two* margaritas as dozens of pterodactyls are swooping in on the attack. As far as I could tell he doesn't spill a drop. Overall though this movie is like something written with a plot wheel: the human characters are total stereotypes (tough but idealistic main guy; frigid workaholic; Greek chorus control-room nerd; two annoying kids who are so insufferable that you'll constantly pray for their deaths even while knowing with 100% certainty that this won't happen). Only the new owner of the park is written/played somewhat against type, if only in the sense that he isn't a *complete* dick. My biggest complaint though is the entire concept of the Gyrosphere. I almost bought it until it was revealed that the guests riding the Gyrosphere control it themselves. Really? So each set of guests can just gyrosphere around a sizable area of Jurassic ~~Park~~ World, in any direction, for as long as they want? And each Gyro only seats two? I sure as hell wouldn't want to be waiting in *that* line. The final insult though is when they break out, as a sideplot, that most eye-rollingly tiresome of sci-fi tropes, the old "let's use this technology to create living weapons" bit, which leads directly into the idiotic fourth act (yes, unlike every other story ever told, this movie felt the need to invent an extra, entirely gratuitous act) wherein they set loose a herd (flock? pod?) of raptors to wipe out the first batch of dinosaurs that are rampaging through the park. Not unlike the time they released cane toads in Australia to wipe out the cane beetle, and with equally disastrous results. Of course, the cane toads weren't led into battle by Star Lord, riding a motorcycle. Seriously, at this point they should've just had the raptors riding motorcycles. It wouldn't have been any noticeably stupider.

King Dinosaur

(1955)

Directed by Bert I. Gordon

A new planet is discovered, so we immediately suit up and make our way there to fuck it up. Drafted for the first mission: an expert on tar pits (hmm, I wonder if they'll encounter a tar pit on this expedition?), a doctor skilled in "treating most diseases and fatalities" (he must be good), and two hot chicks (especially the brunette). Upon landing, our crew encounters what appears to be a nondescript field (probably near the producer's house), filled with stock footage animals. But in-depth atmospheric and chemical testing suggests that it's safe to eat up the running time by aimlessly walking around for several minutes, so that's exactly what they do. Then they take a nap, and later two of them make out (not the girls, unfortunately). So far watching this movie is less interesting than literally anything else you could have spent the same amount of time doing, but, finally, some action: one guy comically rolls down a hill, lands right on top of an alligator, and then easily wrestles it into submission. Okay, so far I can think of two things wrong with the title of this movie. Oops, hold the phone, a giant bug just appeared, and now there's this cute little monkey... So yeah, two things.

Eventually two members of our cast decide to take a boat to this nearby island, and there, finally, they encounter ~~awful, poorly-superimposed footage of an iguana~~ a dinosaur! All right, let me get this straight: it's not enough that these cornheads have journeyed across the cosmos to an alien planet; once there they *still* have to travel to a mysterious, uncharted island to get to the dinosaurs? I'm sorry, but when your movie is only an hour long and the first half is entirely getting-there time-killing filler, maybe it's time to go back to the drawing board. At any rate, the ~~iguana~~ dinosaur comes after them, but then it's attacked by a baby alligator and the two animals in question are goaded into fighting for real. It looks ridiculous and is clearly cruelty to animals, so of course this trick shows up repeatedly in dinosaur movies, even though you could probably portray a more realistic dinosaur fight using cardboard cutouts, shadow puppets, or even just a beloved character actor standing in front of a bookcase and describing the action. Anyway, our heroes manage to escape ~~PETA's wrath~~ the dinosaurs, and then, sensitive to the delicate balance of this unsullied, virgin world, they DESTROY THE ISLAND WITH AN ATOM BOMB. "I brought the atom bomb - I think it's a good time to use it!" says the guy who brought the atom bomb. Reactionary much? Jesus Christ.

Honestly, the only way this movie could be any more 1950s is if those dinosaurs they blew up had been communists.

King Kong

(1966)

Produced by Videocraft International

I've already mentioned the 1978 American cartoon where a middle-class white family summoned Godzilla with a pager whenever they got in a bind ("I'm sorry sir, but we're here to foreclose on your home." "Got to summon GODZILLA!"), but before you judge it too harshly you should know that the Japanese once produced an equally insulting/ridiculous cartoon show about America's own giant monster, King Kong. What I'm saying is, we kinda owed them.

After befriending King Kong in the first episode, this little boy basically keeps him as a pet, which comes in handy whenever he's trapped beneath something heavy (this happens with alarming frequency) or the time his entire family is kidnapped by a Roman centurion-themed volcano cult (King Kong brutally murders the lot of them). Other challenges to pet Kong include a T. rex, a giant squid, aliens, killer bees (which, hilariously, often fly in a gigantic bee-shaped formation), and any number of megalomaniacal imbeciles ("Ever see one of *these*? Of course not; I just invented it!"), including the Lex Luthor to (cartoon) King Kong's Superman, the diabolical *Dr. Who*. (No, the Dr. Who from the *movie*, not the TV show.) (No, from the *King Kong* movie, not the Dr. Who movie.) (No, the *Japanese* King

Kong movie, not the American one.) (Look, just forget it, okay?) All these adventures, and more, are presented in short, six-minute episodes that leave no time for dilly-dallying. Or, you know, quality. The animation is fairly terrible (possibly even worse than the aforementioned Godzilla cartoon, and that one was produced by Hanna-Barbera for fuck's sake), and it's all kinda dumb, but it's still less painful than 2000's *Kong: The Animated Series*, with its tone-deaf "Totally x-treme, dudes!" lingo and all-around 1990s bullshit. Seriously, did anything ever become more instantly dated than crap that was popular in the 1990s?

King Kong

(1976)

Directed by John Guillermin

One reason the original *King Kong* (1933) is such a timeless classic is because the story is saturated with crowd-pleasing, romantic notions. The heroes, for example, are Hollywood filmmakers, once viewed as a highly-glamorous profession. (This was before Jason Friedberg and Aaron Seltzer came along, obviously.) And the main chick gets involved when she's rescued from homeless poverty by said filmmakers and becomes an instant star, something thousands of L.A. waitresses strive for and fail to achieve every single day. This remake tosses all that out the window though. Instead, the jokers in this version are looking for cheap gasoline, making them more akin to your old man, driving all over town looking for that lower price-per-gallon as if the gas and time he's wasting isn't negating the 30 cents he "saves" when he finally does fills up. I think it's time to start looking into homes, seriously.

Despite its reputation (as wall-to-wall shit, basically), the beginning of this flick really isn't so bad, although it is a little distracting that our main guy is The Dude from *The Big Lebowski*, essentially playing the same character (a hippie). It all goes to pot once they reach Dinosaur Island though, because this version omits one very important element: *the goddamn dinosaurs.* I kid you not, there is not a single dinosaur in this entire fucking movie! Who in fuck's name remakes *King Kong* and leaves out the fucking dinosaurs? Without dinosaurs, *King Kong* is just some chick screaming for two hours and a monkey falling off a building, and on a bad day that could be the *B.J. and the Bear* reunion movie. The only hope is that things will pick up when Kong hits the big city, but nope. Oh he busts up this elevated train real good, but after that he just lumbers aimlessly around until the thrilling climax, while The Dude and our main chick eat up the intervening time dealing with their unresolved romance. Ultimately, it ends as it must, with King Kong falling to his death. "'Twas beauty killed the Beast." Or, you know, gravity. One of those two.

King Kong

(2005)

Directed by Peter Jackson

No one has ever had the time to sit through this entire movie.

King Kong Escapes

(1967)

Directed by Ishirô Honda

Believe it or not, this flick is a direct spin-off of the 1966 *King Kong* cartoon (see above), where the mad scientist Dr. Who and Mechani-Kong (the robot version of King Kong) both first appeared. In this take, Dr. Who builds Mechani-Kong to mine a mysterious radioactive element that he plans on selling to some chick so that her country can obtain "nuclear domination of the universe" (wow). Mechani-Kong's Apple-based (I'm assuming) software crashes the first time out though, so Dr. Who is forced to kidnap the real King Kong (AKA "Bong Kong", apparently), hypnotize him, and put *him* to work in the radiation mines. Why didn't Dr. Who simply enslave the real King Kong in the first place? My guess is that he wanted to burn through his allotted robot monster R&D money first, because you know how it is: if he doesn't spend it all he'll get less next year. At any rate, King Kong isn't the sort of monkey who will dance for just anybody, so, as promised, nigga escapes. By now Mechani-Kong is back from the shop though, so Dr. Who sends the robot Kong after the real one and they fight to the finish, by which I mean the end.

Fifty years later I'm still pissed that they never made a sequel where Mechani-Kong fights Mechagodzilla, but that aside his sole cinematic outing is reasonably entertaining. I liked the efficiency of having the weird, chirping noise Mechani-Kong makes double as his theme music, and the little blonde the real King Kong has the hots for is a serious looker. In fact, I'd go so far as to say that she thoroughly trumps original King Kong girl Fay Wray, and I don't suggest this lightly because Fay Wray remains one of the finest chicks who has ever existed, ranking just below Ke$ha and only slightly above Lindsay Lohan.

Hey, it's my book. I'll rank these chippies any way I see fit.

King Kong Lives

(1986)

Directed by John Guillermin

Everything, literally everything, about the 1976 *King Kong* was an unmitigated disaster, which Hollywood generally doesn't have a problem with but I'm pretty sure it lost money too. So why make a sequel? And if I'm wrong and it *did* make money, why make the sequel a *decade* later? Either way, the very existence of this movie makes zero sense, and, as you'll see, they decided to just go ahead and run with that theme.

It's ten years later (Kong time as well as real time), and it seems that the big monkey who breaks everything didn't die when he took a gainer off the World Trade Center after all. He is in a coma though, and he desperately needs a heart transplant because according to this movie your heart is the only thing damaged when you plunge 1368 feet before being stopped by concrete, whereas according to reality your wouldn't even be able to identify his heart because after that kind of catastrophic physical trauma he would most resemble a gigantic gorilla costume filled with soup. Or wait, maybe what they're trying to say, in their own clumsy way, is that after his doomed love affair with the broad from the previous movie his heart is BROKEN. See, it's poignant. Or at least it would be, if that word meant "stupid".

So anyway, the people keeping King Kong alive on the world's biggest respirator (an early use of GoFundMe, no doubt) get a lucky break when Deputy Birdwell Hawkins discovers another giant ape, this one a female, in Borneo. This gives them the plasma they need to operate on King Kong, and, wouldn't you know it, once he's fitted with an artificial heart (in quite possibly the most laughable operation ever captured on film) (not counting the time you got that jar of salsa stuck... up there) both giant monkeys escape. But if you were expecting a typical giant monster rampage x 2, think again. Instead, the two apes just hang out in the hills until they're recaptured, at which point King Kong apparently dies after falling into the river and hitting his head on a rock. Sure, this was tragic when it happened to your drunk cousin, but come on, that's no way for fucking *King Kong* to buy it.

King Kong lives though. (Get it?) (Fuck you, movie.) Seems he's been hiding out in a nearby swamp, subsisting on full-grown alligators (hilariously and unconvincingly played by real, baby alligators). Eventually he's spotted though, at which point some rednecks capture him and try to get him drunk, which goes about as well as you'd imagine. "Oh, Kong. You've killed now," laments the main chick when they find the rednecks' bodies. Uh, he publicly killed tons of people in the previous movie, you dumb bitch. Don't you watch the news? Some more stuff happens, equally stupid, until they wrap it all up with the birth of Baby Kong (sweeping, inspirational music assures us that we aren't supposed to be laughing during this part). King Kong, meanwhile, dies of a heart attack. That's one way to get out of paying the child support, I guess.

King of the Lost World

(2005)

Directed by Leigh Scott

Say what you will about the TV series *Lost* (example: "It was an expertly-mounted hose job that they literally made up as they went along, and I hope 'pulling a *Lost*' becomes a permanent fixture in our lexicon. Screw you, J. J. Abrams."), you have to admit, the plane crash that kicked the whole thing off was pretty badass. Well, this movie – an equal-opportunity ripoff factory that takes on *Lost*, *King Kong* (2005 version) and *Jurassic Park 2* simultaneously – also opens with a plane crash, except in this case it's just one endless stream of embarrassing. And that's *before* the giant cartoon monkey – we'll refer to him as "the Great Grape Ape" – shows up. Pretty soon all sorts of cartoons are attacking the plane crash survivors, although this movie is so poorly made that half the time I couldn't tell which cartoon was supposed to be doing what to whom.

Of course, even the worst cartoon effects are forgivable in the service of a halfway decent story, so it's a good thing that the script itself is a solid, quality piece of work. Ha ha! *Of course* I'm kidding. This script is so retarded that it should be hurling pudding, and it's painfully obvious that the writers (it took more than one) either hold us in utter intellectual contempt or are themselves so jaw-droppingly stupid that the Catholic Church recognizes it as an official miracle when they get through any given day without falling into a hole or accidentally drinking poison. In one part, for example, they try to convince us that a professional airline stewardess wouldn't know the difference between an airliner and a jet fighter! I'm sorry, but I'm pretty sure that "recognizing an airliner" is one of the first things they teach you at professional airline stewardess school. (Amateur airline stewardess school concentrates a lot more on the lap dancing.) Insult me if you must, movie, but I draw the line when you start dissing our lovely, hardworking airline stewardesses. Except for the male ones, of course. Those dinks deserve all the abuse they get.

So anyway, eventually there are only five people left: the aforementioned stewardess, *Scarecrow and Mrs. King* star Bruce Boxliner, a super-hot brunette, a female photographer, and one additional clown who has somehow become the default main guy. The remainder of the movie is just chaotic idiocy and out-of-focus cartoons, so to save time here's what ultimately happens to everyone:

- The stewardess is brainwashed, goes native, and we never see her again. We do see her utterly amazing tits before she vanishes though, and believe me when I say that they will be missed.
- Bruce Boxliner is beaten up by a girl and dies of being beaten up by a girl. Note: he could have avoided this fate simply by fucking her. Queer.
- The Great Grape Ape is blown up with a nuclear

bomb.

- The default main guy, the photographer chick, and the super-hot brunette all survive. He's a fool if he doesn't finagle a threesome out of this.
- Mr. Satanism gets a headache from the out-of-focus cartoon effects and vows to kill anyone who ever puts up money for *King of the Lost World Part 2*. Also J. J. Abrams. Because fuck that guy.

Konga

(1961)

Directed by John Lemont

I'm constantly amazed at what makes the front page of newspapers in the movies. "Doctor Decker Returns". Who? So what? And frankly we'd be better off without this prick: he's dismissive to his special lady friend; he shoots his own cat when it gets into one of his precious mad doctor potions; he cultivates giant Venus flytraps, plus another enormous plant that has a huge, human-looking tongue hanging out of it, like it's constantly funning on Gene Simmons or Miley Cyrus (mad botany, in and of itself, isn't necessarily a bad thing, but let's face it, no one has ever used a giant, meat-eating plant for not evil); he's a dirty old man who macks on chicks half his age, chicks he should be leaving for me; and, finally, he mad-sciences up a killer monkey that he uses to eliminate his ridiculous enemies list, which includes a crotchety old dean, a racist Indian stereotype (7-11, not casino), and a love-sick teenager. The most hilarious aspect of this hopelessly out-to-lunch movie though is that the mad doctor's special lady friend is privy to the majority of his crimes, but has agreed not to turn him in as long as he promises to marry her. Nice priorities, whore. Okay, so she does have her doubts, briefly losing it over breakfast one morning ("What are you having with your poached egg? *Murder?*"), but she doesn't actually turn on him until she catches him pawing all over some sweet young thing in his killer plant greenhouse. That's when she feeds the homicidal monkey an extra helping of growth formula, at which point it swells to King Kong proportions and goes on a short (< 12 minutes) rampage. In the end the monkey dies, the scientist dies, the special lady friend dies, and the fate of the sweet young thing is left unresolved, as the last we saw of her she was getting her arm gnawed off by a gigantic plant.

Dated and corny, even by the relatively lax standards of the 1940s. This had no business being made in 1961.

Kong Island

(1968)

Directed by Robert Morris

If one cat in your gang ruthlessly shoots everyone else in the gang, that's the cat you probably shouldn't turn your back on, idiot. Our main guy survives being shot in the back though, and when he finds out that his treacherous former partner is somehow mixed up in a gorilla mind-control scheme (don't ask) you better believe he volunteers to go after the dude. Much walking around in the jungle ensues, and a lot of people die, but it's all pretty boring, even with the hostile natives, the ugly jungle goddess, ample double-dealing, and the classic if predictable climax in which the gorillas turn on their master while his second-hand circa-1940 mad scientist equipment explodes all around him.

A useless movie any way you look at it. Even the title is a misnomer. The action doesn't take place anywhere near an island.

Lancelot Link: Secret Chimp

(1970)

Created by Mike Marmer and Stan Burns

Even given our current no-end-in-sight spate of senseless reality programming and ancient alien Kardashians, *Get Smart* (1965-1970) remains one of the worst television shows ever created. It consisted of exactly three jokes (the Cone of Silence, the shoe phone, and the main guy saying "Missed it by THAT much."), repeated over and over and over again for *five fucking seasons* until we were all so sick of it that we wanted to cram that shoe phone right down the producers' throats, while simultaneously cramming our face up co-star Agent 99's twat because let's face it, she was pretty damn hot. And you'd think five seasons of this brain-rot crap would be enough for said producers, no matter how much they hated the general public, but oh no, it turns out that two of the cocksuckers behind *Get Smart* took it one hate-fuck further and made an entirely new version of the show *starring talking monkeys*. That's right, this show features real-life chimpanzees engaged in approximations of unfunny spy adventures, and it's all just as ghastly as it sounds. The main chimp's entire shtick consists of an endless Humphrey Bogart impersonation (an unusually specific but verifiable trend in children's programming - there was an orangutan in the 1980s cartoon *Shirt Tales* that tormented us with a perpetual Bogart impression too), the jokes are either puns or nonexistent, and it all serves no purpose whatsoever except to allow the detestable swine who produced it to engage in their own little monkey boning party, figuratively speaking of course. Also, I am totally accusing them of literally having sexual intercourse with the monkeys. Watching *Lancelot Link* is like drowning in a gutter filled with the blood of puppies and betrayed heroes. If you have even a sliver of taste or empathy for your fellow man, every single frame of this intellectual abortion will have you frothing with rage, and the fact that people were paid actual, non-Monopoly money to create it is a crime against humanity that I think I can say, without hyperbole, rivals the Holocaust, assuming of course that the Holocaust took place on the Planet of the Apes and this is what the ape Nazis watched on television afterwards. Okay, I'm so pissed off here that I've stopped making sense; I'm literally incoherent with rage. Fuck you, *Lancelot Link*. Pray to your gods for forgiveness, creators Mike Marmer and Stan Burns, you evil, inhuman fucks. History will judge you far more harshly than I.

The Land Before Time VIII: The Big Freeze

(2001)

Directed by Charles Grosvenor

It wasn't so bad when there were only a couple of these smarmy-ass *Land Before* fucking *Time* movies, but by the time Part 6 (6!) rolled around I really wanted to see the baby dinosaurs who serve as the main characters just grow up and eat each other already, or, failing that, be struck dead by the hand of God since every good Christian knows that dinosaurs were invented by the Devil to test our faith. Not unlike Lady Gaga's ass. So yeah, I was definitely pumped for this "big freeze" to finally put Littlefoot and his irritating friends out of my misery. My favorite moment in this entire series is when the baby dinosaurs engage in a spirited snowball fight, not realizing that, as reptiles, the cold will soon slow their metabolisms to a crawl, rampant cell death will occur, ice crystals will form inside their bodies, and they'll all die lingering, agonizing deaths. (Thank you, Animal Planet.) Unfortunately, that's not what happens, and [number too high to express without complicated mathematics] additional, blasphemous *Land Before Times* (*Lands Before Time*?) followed. Oh well, at least we manage to make it almost ten minutes into this one before the dinosaurs belt out their first crappy, unmemorable song. It's about being angry. How appropriate.

Land of the Lost

(2009)

Directed by Brad Silberling

When it comes to old TV shows, sometimes you just have to accept that shit at face value. Maybe collision insurance simply isn't available in Hazzard County. Maybe that little black kid will never quite grasp what anyone is talkin' 'bout. When it comes to rebooting old TV shows though, Hollywood's go-to is almost always the ironic, patronizing dick approach, even when the show in question was actually pretty good. Take Sid & Marty Krofft's *Land of the Lost*, for example. Sure, the dinosaurs were hand puppets and I think the crystals inside the mysterious pylons that controlled the place were re-purposed Ring Pops, but it was a legitimately good show, like seriously smart science fiction. It was certainly no worse than say, goddamned one-note *Planet of the Apes*, or even the original *Star Trek*, where every other alien race based their entire culture on a cheesy genre film. Hell, *Star Trek*'s Chekov even *wrote* an episode of *Land of the Lost*, not that he's proud of it or anything, as evidenced by the dismissive, condescending commentary track he provided for the Season 1 DVD box set. Dude, you're fucking *Chekov;* I'm pretty sure your job on the *Enterprise* was making the coffee. You've got zero foundation for being such a self-important douchebag. This is why, whenever I see Chekov jockeying a table at a nerd convention, I always make a big scene and start yelling "Hey! It's SULU from the Original Series! Everyone come get an autograph from SULU!" Seriously, you have no idea how much this pisses him off. Fuck you, Chekov, you coffee-brewing dick. You're nothing.

That's exactly the sort of attitude I'm talking about though, and it's painfully apparent in the *Land of the Lost* movie, which immediately plays the "too cool for" card, bringing in Will Ferrell to Anchorman up the place with his Anchorman bullshit. (Seriously, besides *Elf*, has Will Ferrell *ever* been in a good movie?) As a result, what could've been a genuinely cool sci-fi adventure instead features Chaka the monkey boy repeatedly grabbing the main chick's tits (not that I blame him), Will Ferrell drinking piss, and so on and so forth. I was ready to hate the fuck out of this movie, and probably beat my girlfriend after it was over, but in an amazing second-act twist it turns out that some of their irreverent dickery is actually passably funny. The main characters' reaction to the vibrating pylons ("Holly, you should sit on this.") that are bigger on the inside than on the outside ("It's like Snoopy's doghouse."), for example, are especially hilarious, but the only people who will really get it are folks who loved the original show but don't mind that they're making fun of it, and I'm guessing that those vectors barely intersect. Most of the gags are pretty dumb and/or involve being expelled out of anuses though, so in the end watching *Will Ferrell's Land of the Lost* isn't so much a positive experience as one that isn't quite as negative as you'd feared. Like thinking you have AIDS, but finding out it's only the clap.

The Land that Time Forgot

(1975)

Directed by Kevin Connor

You know who can suck it? Everyone, because despite its bad reputation with just about everybody this is the best goddamned dinosaur movie ever made, bar none and fuck you. It starts with some World War Part 1 proto-Nazis torpedoing a civilian ship, solely to be dicks, after which they surface only to have their entire sub seized by the shell-shocked survivors. Ah, the German military, is there anything they do that doesn't begin with devastating ruthlessness and end in abject, embarrassing failure? This is only the first of several mutinous uprisings though, and before long this goddamn submarine has changed hands more times than a clean, fifteen-year-old whore on Free Whore Day. As a result, everyone gets confused and they end up in the South Atlantic, where they discover a Lost World inhabited by unspeakably cool-looking dinosaurs that want to eat them. (Okay, fine, the pterodactyls look like something pilfered from a baby's mobile, but the rest of the dinos are unspeakably cool, trust me.) Some distinction is achieved with a wild "evolution is really freaky here" sideplot, there's a scene where the main guy kicks a caveman who's drowning in quicksand in the face and then tries to use his head as a stepping stone ("Oog not your stepping stone!"), and the token chick is played by Susan Penhaligon, arguably the hottest piece of ass going in 1975. It's practically blasphemy that she never gets naked. (She does get naked in a 1974 movie called *Soft Beds, Hard Battles* though, so you should definitely check that one out.) If I were your typical movie critic, I would declare this flick "a triumph." I'm not that gay though, so lets all just agree that it kicks fucking ass.

Followed by a bullshit sequel.

The Land that Time Forgot

(2009)

Directed by C. Thomas Howell

How in fuck's name can you film *The Land that Time Forgot* and leave out all the fighting over the submarine? In the original novel, half the goddamned plot was taken up with people fighting over the submarine; the christing thing changes hands so many times it could be a drinking game. That aside, the beginning of this version isn't too bad; they play it really close to the dick for a while and as a result it's all kind of mysterious and creepy. It doesn't take them long to ass it all up though. First off, it turns out that the jokers in this movie haven't discovered a Lost World of dinosaurs at all, they've actually traveled back in time. So it's not really "the land that time forgot" then, is it? Duh. Even ignoring that, it's pretty hard to take a movie seriously when it includes lines like "I'll lead you right to it. Can't promise it's still there though." (What?) Or when it features a scene where a T. rex just spontaneously explodes for no reason. (I know they shot a torpedo at it, but apparently the drunk in charge of the cartoon effects forgot to actually paste that torpedo in there.) And speaking of, they shortchange us on the dinosaurs too - we really only see three, and two of them are the same kind. What a half-baked turd. The only plus is the brunette: she's amazing, and her legs are far and away the best special effect in this entire movie. Like the stunner in the 1975 version though, she never does get naked. It might as well be the Land that Tits Forgot.

The Land Unknown

(1957)

Directed by Virgil Vogel

A military expedition to *Neu-Schwabenland*, er, I mean *Antarctica*, discovers a mysterious canyon populated with dinosaurs. But what starts as a rousing old-school adventure ("rousing" being the required nomenclature when discussing old-school adventures) crashes headfirst into suckville when we finally see the dinosaurs, because aside from one mechanical plesiosaur (which is very cool) the rest of the dinos consist of 1) real lizards goaded into fighting one another and 2) an undocumented Mexican lumbering around in a T. rex suit so half-assed that it looks like someone's kids made it. And this from Universal, the movie studio that previously invented the original Frankenstein, Wolf Man, Mummy, etc., all of which were groundbreaking for their time. It's pretty embarrassing. Other threats include a carnivorous plant (which, I'm happy to report, eats the "cute" proto-monkey our heroes adopt before it has the chance to become too cloying) and a modern-day rapist who somehow found his way into the canyon previously and as a result might be the only human being truly living off the grid. Eat your heart out, Ed Begley Jr. With the introduction of the rapist a conflict over the expedition's sole chick naturally arises (she pretends to be upset about this, but you know she was loving every minute of it), but in the end everyone settles their differences and they all manage to escape from Dinosaur Canyon without a single fatality. In other words, fucking weak.

The Last Dinosaur

(1977)

Directed by Alex Grasshoff and Tom Kotani

His name is "Masten Thrust". He has his own James Bond-style theme song (even if it is somewhat him-deprecating). He knows how to smooth-talk the ladies whilst simultaneously showing them no respect whatsoever. (Actual Masten Thrust pickup line: "I keep wondering what your muff would taste like.") His hobby is shooting endangered species. In short, when Dos Equis' Most Interesting Man in the World cries like a bitch on another man's shoulder and then drunkenly sucks his dick, that shoulder, and dick, belong to Masten Thrust. So naturally when a Lost World full of prehistoric monsters is discovered he's the first in line to kill every last one of them and then hate-fuck their steaming carcasses whilst chugging 40-year-old scotch straight from the bottle and using his other hand to fist Jacqueline Bisset. Unfortunately, that's not quite how it works out. Instead, Thrust and his party end up stranded in the Lost World, where they proceed to spend most of the remaining running time lollydicking around and squabbling with the local cavemen. The old-school monsters are too cheap and rubbery, even for me (the pterodactyls are especially wretched); the Wile E. Coyote number Thrust and company pull on the T. rex is pretty hard to swallow; and they use the same overly-dramatic musical sting to underscore *everything,* whether it suits the action or not. (Kick that campfire!) The worst thing about this movie though? The main chick. It's one thing to cast some thirtysomething, Driving Miss Daisy hag as your main chick, and another thing entirely to have her constantly vamping it up à la Blanche Devereaux on *The Golden Girls.* God help us, it's the *Star Trek V* Uhura fan dance, all over again. Seriously, you'll probably lose your lunch.

The "Legend of Dinosaurs"

(1977)

Directed by Junji Kurata

Okay, what's with the quotation marks around most, but not all, of the title? Is there some ironic angle I'm not privy to? Seriously, movie, what's the gag? Stop messing with my head.

Old-school Japanese dinosaurs ("regular" ones, not Godzilla-sized), discovered in a hole by a cute, barefoot chick (calm down, Joss Whedon), go on an uncharacteristically gory rampage-jamboree. A horse is decapitated, a plesiosaur bisects a scuba cutie and shows its disdain for pranksters, and a pterodactyl carries a guy off and then drops him to his death while hilariously inappropriate jazz music plays. Plus: some almost-nudity, a bitch gets slapped around, two dinosaurs fight, and more. Okay, not much more. Truth be told, I just hit most of the highlights in a movie that has far too many dead spots and could've used a lot more action. Still, what it does deliver is acceptably awesome, and only a humorless outrage addict who licks their fingers after they wipe could really find anything bad to say about it. Sadly, those people are out there. Have you seen some of the reviews of my first book?

Link

(1986)

Directed by Richard Franklin

Nineteen-eighties touchstone hottie Adventures in Babysitting vs. a homicidal, pyromaniac orangutan? I am so on board, because there is no way this won't be entertaining. If it's good, well, then it's good. But if it's bad it'll be hilarious, and if it's *really* bad, who knows how far they'll go? Hell, we might just see one of the finest babes of the 1980s sexually assaulted by a monkey, which isn't something I woke up today wanting to see, but now that the idea is kinda out there anyway...

Okay, there's no non-creepy place to go with this, so let's just skip ahead to the plot.

A in B is assisting one of her professors with his primate research, confident that she can handle the gig because, as she explains, she "used to babysit", which would be a cute in-joke except for the fact that *Link* came out one year before *Adventures in Babysitting*, relegating it to "weird coincidence". As it turns out, our semi-mad doctor's research is being conducted not at the college but at his isolated pad, and when one of the monkeys turns out to be sociopathic *and* much smarter than the average bear, or monkey, you can easily guess where this one is going. Believe it or not though, *Link* is actually a pretty good movie: scenes of the orangutan killing a guard dog, busting up through the floor, and wasting the inevitable third-act morons who drop by for a visit are handled realistically enough to be scary instead of hilarious (they're still hilarious, of course, but, you know, in a good way); a few parts are legitimately disturbing (like the bit where the orangutan coolly and overtly ogles a naked A in B like he wants to tap that primo ass just as much as we do); and of course A in B looks fantastic, especially with her clothes off (thank you, movie gods). My only complaints are the ridiculous "Top of the world, Ma!" ending and the part where the orangutan surprise-grabs one dork and pulls him into a well. Seriously, it's broad fucking daylight and this dork was staring right into that well. How did he not see an entire orangutan hiding in there?

Lost Continent

(1951)

Directed by Samuel Newfield

The military misplaces its brand new missile (your tax dollars at work), and the retrieval team they send after it discovers more than they bargained for: an all-but-inaccessible mountaintop inhabited by... ah, hell, it's just a little ol' lizard. Talk about anti-climactic. Seriously, this flick was actually building up rather nicely until they sprung that lizard on us. For the first "dinosaur" the audience sees, the one that really needs to wow us, couldn't they have built a big puppet or at the very least enlisted their best drawer to sketch it on a piece of paper? Anything would've been better than filming one of the exact same lizards my cat Mr. Meowgi is always killing and leaving on the front stoop and trying to pass it off as a prehistoric monster. Hell, at the *very least* they could have super-composed a person into the shot and used some forced perspective to make the lizard LOOK big, so that we at least understood what we're *supposed* to be looking at. I'm not exaggerating when I say that this single shot of a harmless little lizard torpedoes *Lost Continent* entirely. It literally goes from being a grand, epic adventure to a being a laughable farce in one second flat.

But a movie is like a marriage: just because you've given up on it doesn't mean it ends. Our heroes eventually make it to the very top of the mountain, at which point everything is suddenly tinted green, kind of like how *The Wizard of Oz* switches from black & white to full color but, obviously, considerably chintzier. The dinosaurs they find there are pretty chintzy too, but at least they look like actual (fake) dinosaurs. They're too little, too late, though, and frankly it's pretty pathetic that even the best of them look so much worse than the dinosaurs in *King Kong* (1933), which was made like a generation earlier. And then there's the closing line, trying to be all self-important and deep but only succeeding at being utterly nonsensical. "Lost" continent? More like hopeless.

The Lost Tribe

(2009)

Directed by Roel Reiné

Early in this movie this guy tells his girlfriend of three years how wonderful she is, then gives her a box that looks like it would have a ring inside. Instead, it's a key. To his heart? To the house he bought for them to live in together? To a much larger box containing a ring so big that it will make her collapse in a dead faint during which she shits herself but they'll obviously leave that part out when they tell the story later? Nope, he's just asking her to move in with him, and it's the key to his crummy studio apartment or whatever. Now, I've been married three times, and as a consequence I am the most unromantic guy in the history of ever, but even I think this cat deserves to be kicked in the balls for that one.

Anyway, the actual story begins when Lieutenant Romance and his friends, who are out making business deals on a boat (yes, I instantly hated them too), pull this fuckhole out of the drink, after which said fuckhole proceeds to crash said boat into an island. You're supposed to go around those, idiot. Stranded full-on Gilligan style, they're utterly fucked when they're attacked by a tribe of missing links who, for some reason, only see things in black & white. You know, like FOX News. Okay, I can accept the premise that there are still some missing links out there (I've been to Jersey), but this movie totally lost me with the cretin idea that the Catholic church would want to destroy all evidence of this because the existence of a missing link proves that there is no God, because a) no it doesn't and b) as a general rule, the Catholics are way more concerned about eating meat on the wrong day of the week than evolution. Besides, this whole "evolution busters" sideplot goes absolutely noplace anyway, so why did they even bother to include it? Oh, and this is hardly an observation exclusive to this movie, but just once I'd like to see someone jump off a cliff into a river in a last ditch effort to escape, only for the river to be just a few inches deep, so that they break both their legs, telescope their spine, and then drown. You could've been the movie that finally granted me this wish, *The Lost Tribe*. Instead, you failed me again.

So yeah, this flick definitely sucks. Yet for some inexplicable reason I can't quite find it in myself to rant and rave and entirely lose my shit over it. Call it... the lost diatribe.

The Lost World

(1925)

Directed by Harry O. Hoyt

A loony professor is rounding up people to accompany him on a dinosaur hunt. Reporters need not apply, however. (Also the Irish.) (Probably.) So when one guy who wants to join up admits that he is, in fact, a reporter, the professor attacks him! Later the reporter stops by the prof's house to try to smooth things over, but the professor just attacks him again! The professor eventually gives in through, the reporter joins the team, and they're off. Now, as you can imagine, some real weirdos have signed up for this magic carpet ride (who goes on a dinosaur hunt wearing blackface?), but the member of this expedition that most stands out in my mind, for all the wrong reasons, is actually their mascot, the monkey:

I mean my god, he looks like he's about to get the beating of a lifetime, and knows it. What have they been doing to this poor bastard? Whatever it is, payback is a bitch - I'm pretty sure the monkey at least partly responsible when the party's log bridge is compromised, trapping them on the mountain where all the dinosaurs live. With plenty of trees on hand why they can't simply make another log bridge is a mystery, but it probably has something to do with the fact that they really are complete idiots. They do manage to escape eventually though, and a Brontosaurus just happens to fall off the mountain at the same time (this part's hilarious), so they're able to capture it and take it back to the big city, which, if you've ever seen any movie ever, you already know is a bad idea. (Of course, this was one of the first movies ever made, so these clowns can be excused for not having that frame of reference.) It would've been nice if the tag-along flapper chick took off her top at some point (trust me, flapper chicks were known to do this), and there's no gore, but there is enough dinosaur-fueled chaos and destruction that, even sans sound or color (or tits), it's still the most watchable version of this movie anyone's made yet, despite being nearly 100 years old. Which is pretty sad, when you think about it.

The Lost World

(1960)

Directed by Irwin Allen

There's no shortage of cinematic bastardizations of Sir Arthur "Savage Sword of Conan" Doyle's novel *The Lost World* (first published in 1912), and like most of them this one begins when a cranky old professor insists that he's discovered living, breathing dinosaurs on an inaccessible plateau, prompting his colleagues to mount (heh) an expedition to check it out, if for no other reason than to get him out of their hair for a while. Now, you'd think they'd enlist a bunch of scientists and big-game hunters for an venture like this, maybe hire a few ex-Marines or ninjas for added protection. But nope, these halfwits select, as two examples, a chick in tight pink pants (who brings along her ugly little dog, which she carries around in a basket full-on Paris Hilton style) and a singing helicopter pilot. And these are a couple of their saner choices. At least the helicopter pilot is good for getting them to the plateau, but once there the helicopter is wrecked by a gigantic lizard. (The "professor" calls it a Brontosaurus, but any fool can see that it's just a garden-variety lizard, albeit considerably larger than most. Did anyone even check this guy's credentials?) Everyone wanders around for a while, they pick up a hot native chick, a giant green spider puts the "special needs" in "special effects", and two more dinosaurs turn up and fight each other. These "dinosaurs" are, once again, just a big lizard and a baby crocodile covered with flair and goaded into fighting for real, a trick that was old hat even in 1960 and is only entertaining if you're the type of person who enjoys cockfighting or tying two cats' tails together and then throwing them over a clothesline. (My editor wanted me to warn any kids who might be reading not to try the cat thing, like kids today even know what a "clothesline" is.) In the end everyone is forced to escape through the volcano (of course there's a volcano), which leads to this movie's best/most hilarious moment: someone falling into lava, represented by a laughably fake puppet being thrown into clearly not-lava. There's no nudity, and only one person is eaten by a dinosaur. It's a pretty sorry movie.

The Lost World

(1992)

Directed by Timothy Bond

Need an intolerable blowhard for your movie? Would it help if he was fat, too? Look no further than John Rhys-Davies, best known for playing Indiana Jones' sidekick in *Raiders of the Lost Ark*, the fat guy in *Sliders*, and an insufferable dick in pretty much everything else. And what is with his hyphenated last name, anyway? Is he married to another dude? If that's the case it's okay with me, but I'll bet it's not. I'll bet he does it because it makes him feel superior. "I have *two* last names, sir, while other, more *common* men, merely have *one*." Christ, I can totally hear him saying that. What an ass trophy.

Plot-wise it's the same basic story as every other adaptation of *The Lost World* (see above, and below), although the specifics are somewhat stupider than usual. Take the reporter, for example: he's so fucking gullible that all it takes to convince him that an unknown land populated by dinosaurs might really exist is a pencil sketch of a Lost World sunset made by someone who had supposedly been there. Jesus fucking Christ, *there aren't even any dinosaurs in the sketch!* They also add a young boy to the proceedings, which would be fine if he was just another redshirt whose *raison d'eaten* was to be gobbled up by one of the dinosaurs, the preferred fate of any child appearing in a dinosaur movie. (Take the hint, *Jurassic Park* series.) That's not what happens though, so why they bothered to include him is a mystery, unless it's because à la *South Park* only a child could get away with being so fucking racist: "I saw an ape! Or a man. A little of both, actually," he says after spying a perfectly normal-looking black guy. Why couldn't one of the dinosaurs have eaten him, again? The dinosaurs themselves, meanwhile, are a mixed bag. Some – like the pterodactyl that attacks the guy in the subterranean cave – are pretty damned cool, while others are so cheesy and cutesy that I half expected them to suddenly burst into a song about state capitals or how to conjugate your verbs or something. Screw that jazz. If I wanted cute, I'd call Disney. Or better yet, Ariana Grande. Any chick who appeared on a *kids' show* as a character named "Cat Valentine" (essentially, "Pussy Love") is a chick I need to meet.

The Lost World

(1998)

Directed by Bob Keen

This take on Arthur Conan Doyle's perennial public domain favorite starts with a Chinaman being eaten by a swarm of killer bats. Hey, he who lives by the teeming hordes, dies by the teeming hordes, am I right? From here though it's a good half hour before our principal cast finds their way to the Lost World, more than enough time for me to realize that I hated the lot of them, mainly for their infuriating tendency to make stupid, dangerous decisions when other, saner options are readily available. Case in point (and this is the big one, since it kind of invalidates the entire movie): the main guy's motivating factor in locating the Lost World is to prove that dinosaurs didn't really die out millions of years ago, but everyone seems to overlook the fact that the whole idea came about after he came into possession of an only-recently-deceased baby dinosaur. Hell, he breaks the thing out right in the middle of the big press conference where he proposes the trip! So he's proposing a highly dangerous and extremely expensive expedition into lands unknown to prove that dinosaurs still exist, *when he literally has that very proof in a jar right in front of him*. Sounds like an investment scam to me.

So it all makes zero sense, but there are a few clever bits along the way. The first "Lost World" creatures they encounter are disease-carrying mosquitoes, a nice, realistic touch. The part where the chick is abducted is a good jump-scare moment. And, if you're patient, there is some gore. All told, a passable adventure, but nothing to get excited about.

Nothing to get... *excited*... about.

So really, that means it's not a very good *adventure* movie at all, is it? You know what the real problem here is? I've gone soft, and it's high time for that to change. So FUCK this lackluster coprolite of a movie - there's no tits, the plot is nonsensical dogshit, and too many of the dinosaurs are cartoons that look like crap, especially the baby Centrosaurus that the guy-who's-obviously-gonna-betray-them picks up at one point. I swear, it looks like it was cut & pasted in by someone who forgot to check the "lossless compression" box. And don't even get me started on another character's slapsticky death-by-balloon, which probably wasn't meant to be as laugh-out-loud funny as I found it but damn it, it just fucking was. And that, I think it's safe to say, was the high point of *this* stupid-ass flick. Fuck you, *The Lost World 1998*. You can suck my dick.

The Lost World: The Adventure Begins

(1999)

Directed by Richard Franklin

A Great White Hunter type hears cannibal drums. His reaction? He rubs poison all over himself! Needless to say that's fucking awesome, and it looked like things might finally be on track for one of these *Lost World* adaptations, right up to the point where Sheena, Queen of the Jungle shows up and invites the explorers into her all-mod-cons tree house that has everything but high-speed Internet service. Of course she speaks English, and she taught one of the natives to speak it too, which seems kind of pointless until you remember that circa 1912 it didn't matter how inaccessible and exotic your land and people were, it was only a matter of time before the British showed up and started wreaking the place. Best to be able to beg for mercy in a language they can understand. The first big dinosaur reveal is a bit too reminiscent of *Jurassic Park*, but I'll give them a pass on that since they do trot out a wider-than-usual range of threats for our heroes to contend with, including man-eating plants and huge caterpillars with sulfuric acid for blood. (Er, why stab it then?) Their biggest advantage (besides guns, and writer's fiat of course): the hot air balloon they came in, which they use to survey the landscape and swoop down on terrified ape men. They never use the balloon to simply escape though, constantly begging the locals for the location of an apocryphal tunnel that supposedly leads back to the foot of the plateau where the Lost World is located. JUST FLOAT DOWN IN THE BALLOON, YOU DUMBASSES. Jesus Christ, it's not rocket science. Okay, it's flight, so it's like the precursor to rocket science, making it an appropriate-to-them contemporary parallel, but you know what I mean.

This kicked off an utterly ridiculous TV series featuring everything from giant hypnosis bees to time travel, and if it wasn't the primary inspiration for shit-merchant J.J. Abrams' even-stupider *Lost*, I'll eat ~~my hat~~ your girlfriend's pussy.

The Lost World

(2001)

Directed by Stuart Orme

A canoe runs hilariously aground, totally knocking a native guide the fuck out. Ha ha! What a great start to... well, anything, actually. Seriously, if this was day one of my tropical vacation, I would be ecstatic. Unless of course I was in the same canoe and, as a result, spilled some of my overpriced fruity-alcohol beverage. Funny is funny, but even I have my limits.

So anyway, this particular guide is working for Lou Grant imitator Bob Hoskins, who's been in fucking everything but almost no one realizes this because they always assume it's Lou Grant. Bob has located some live dinosaurs, so he returns to civilization, makes a scene, and recruits several bozos to go back with him and catch one. As expected, they end up stranded in dinosaur land, this time due to the treachery of TV's Columbo, who's a Christian so *of course* he betrays them. (Columbo, incidentally, is a surprisingly shitty actor for someone who's been at this game since the late 1950s. Watching him flail around like an amped-up spazmo is, frankly, pretty embarrassing.)

As we've seen, this story has been told so many times, and like every other version this one is as prudish and Victorian as the original source material, which at least had the excuse of actually being written within a few years of Victorian times. Seriously, people, this was made in 2001; how's about a dollop of sleaze to jazz things up a bit? I sure wouldn't have minded seeing the main chick's tits, for example, or at least her ass. She's got kind of a stealth hotness going on, but trust me, she's fucking hot. (Okay, to be fair this chick does strip down to her – I guess those would be her "bloomers" – to go for a swim at one point. It's not much, but trust me, it would've been pretty racy stuff in your great-great-great-great-grandfather's day.) The pacing, meanwhile, is way too slow, and entirely too much time is spent dicking around with these asshole cave apes and a tribe of Wild West Indians who inexplicably show up from an entirely different movie to hang out. Oh, and the ending, a perfect storm of anti-climax, cliché, and dumb ("Someone has sent me a rather interesting map...") is officially one of the worst on record. In the plus column (this will be a very short sentence): a smidgen of gore (blink/fall asleep from boredom, and you'll miss it), and the dinosaur effects aren't half bad, a mixture of passable cartoons and cool puppets, similar to the effects in the BBC documentary series *Walking with Dinosaurs*. Which makes sense, because this movie was also produced by the BBC. In fact, they even borrow some observations from *Walking with Dinosaurs*, like the "fact" that dinosaurs are repelled by the smell of poop. Okay, really, how could anyone possibly know this? It's obvious you're just making half this stuff up, Science, and you know what? Two can play at that game. I say that dinosaurs *liked* the smell of poop. I say they liked it so much that they ate poop all the time. Oh oh - it's a scientific controversy! Batten the hatches!

Hide your daughters! Don't get buried alive beneath all the monocles popping out of stuffy old men's eyes! Give me a fucking break, Science. You're nothing but a bunch of bullshit artists.

And the same goes for you, Religion, times a million.

Mammoth

(2006)

Directed by Tim Cox

"Killer mammoth" is a hard sell, because no matter how you spin it it will always boil down to Snuffleupagus trampling people to death, and while I wouldn't say that nobody wants to see that, I'm fairly certain that nobody wants to see it over and over again for 90 minutes. Fortunately, the cats who made *Mammoth* realized this, so they sprinkled some *Horror Express* in there and the next thing you know we've got an *alien-possessed* mammoth using its trunk to literally suck the life out of people, before trampling whatever's left. Rounding out the experience: a little gore, an FBI agent sporting a rack that just made *my* most wanted list, and, best of all, River from *Firefly* as the main chick. (If you aren't familiar with *Firefly*, that's River Tam, not River Phoenix.) I was a little disappointed that River never takes her clothes off, but I'll let it slide because I'd rather see her in a t-shirt and jeans than most other chicks naked. She's that fine. *Mammoth* is no classic, but over the years a disproportionate number of Sci-Fi/Syfy/Syphilis Channel movies whose titles start with the letter M (*Mansquito, Manticore, Mandrake, Marknado 2*) have clocked in at well above average, and this is yet another entry in that bizarrely narrowly-focused list. Clearly the universe is trying to tell us something, but as to what that might be, well, your guess is as good as mine. Ha ha! I'm totally kidding: my guess is way better than yours. See, M is Roman for 1000, and the Romans killed Jesus, so crunch the numbers and you'll get the exact number of millenniums before Jesus comes back and kicks everyone's ass. So yeah, I'd start stocking up on the ramen if I were you. Roman ramen, if you can find it. Ha ha! Roman ramen! From Donald Rumsfeld's Roman Ramen and Rum Cake Emporium! It's the bees' knees! Too bad they're *killer* bees. Don't think they're not plugged in, though: *Killer bee, killer bee, killer bee, killer bee... speaking words of wisdom, killer bee.* Lennon and McCartney were totally in on it, man. Not Ringo though; he just drove the moped.

Addendum: Okay, full disclosure: I kinda-sorta ate like a year's recommended allowance of shrooms right before I reviewed *Mammoth* here. At first I thought that I should probably go back and revamp this entry, but I dunno, it looks like I spelled everything right, and except for that Jesus/Rumsfeld stuff at the end all the facts seem to check out. I mean, do I really want to sit through *Mammoth* again? Best to move forward. Besides, the next movie has a cave bear in it, and I love me some cave bears.

Master of the World

(1983)

Directed by Alberto Cavallone

There's a lot more caveman porn out there than you would imagine (okay, maybe not YOU, but more than normal people would imagine), but this is the only caveman gore movie I'm aware of, and from a gruesome violence standpoint, at least, it leaves contemporaries like *Clan of the Cave Bear*, *Quest for Fire*, and *Yor: The Hunter from the Future* (hey, I needed a third one, okay?) in the dust. See, those movies were all based on books, so, with their "importance" firmly established, they were perfectly content to bore our dicks off. This movie, on the other hand, prefers to kick them off, with a side-helping of karate chop to the throat. People are decapitated; brains are eaten; tail-wagging wolves attack (Who's a good boy? Who's a *good boy?*); a moth-eaten bear mauls a guy up and then wanders drunkenly around in the background, like it missed its cue or something (later, another guy channels Leslie Nielsen and attacks this bear bare-handed); there are endless assaults via rock, pointy stick, and what appears to be the jawbone of an ass (how *profound*); and, if you watch carefully, there's even some beaver. Yes, it's annoying and stupid (sample dialogue: "Ah ahh ahhh ahh ah uh uh uh uhn ah ahh ah uhn uh uh uh!"), and it's fucking boring, but at least none of the Beatles are in it, and it ends with a nuclear explosion, which makes no goddamned sense whatsoever but it's nice to know there won't be a sequel. (Unless they go and *Conquest of the Planet of the Apes* us, which I wouldn't put past them.) My only real complaint is that, from beginning to end, I had no idea what these goddamn cavemen were constantly fighting about, making it all but impossible to relate to any of them. Except for the ones who subsequently ate their opponents, of course. At least I knew where they were coming from.

Mighty Joe Young

(1949)

Directed by Ernest B. Schoedsack

"It's got to be something different, something original," demands a guy early in this movie. That's pretty fucking ironic, because this is yet *another* flick about a giant gorilla produced by the one-note Johnny who gave us *King Kong*, *Son of Kong*, *Lawyer of Kong*, and fuck knows how many other diminishing-return giant gorilla movies the world has since forgotten. When they point out that half of all movies made before 1950 are lost, trust me, sometimes that's a good thing.

Alright, so *this* giant ape is peacefully kicking it in Africa – where he's the kinda-sorta pet of a young woman with terrible, terrible eyebrows – when he's "discovered" by a promoter who immediate sends a bunch of honest-to-ass cowboys to "recruit" him for the nightclub circuit. And I have to say, the big cowboy-gorilla brouhaha that results is pretty entertaining. (You don't see a lot of cowboys vs. gorilla scenes in the movies, which is why Hollywood needs to swallow its balls already and cough up for my latest screenplay: *The Good, the Bad, and the Planet of the Apes*.) The cowboys lose though, forcing the promoter to switch to his contingency plan: asking nicely. Thoroughly smitten, Eyebrows agrees to escort her giant gorilla to the big city, where he's immediately cast in a live show that consists almost entirely of people punching and/or throwing things at him. Nope, I can't see *this* ending badly. Amazingly enough there are no real problems though, at least until these jokers decide to get the gorilla drunk, at which point he goes bananas (heh) and tears up the club. Here's the best part though: this movie takes place in the days before "public safety" was really a thing, so this just happens to be a lion-themed nightclub, featuring real lions, which the giant gorilla ends up fighting in what is inarguably the best part of the movie. (The producers were so dedicated to this scene, in fact, that at one point it looks like they hoisted a *real lion* into the air so they could drop it several feet right through a goddamned table. Take that, PETA.) Soon Mighty Joe Young is on the loose, but before they can call in the World War Part 1 flying aces to take him out once and for all he does a sudden about-face and saves a baby from a burning building. And never mind all the people (and lions) he killed previously, this isolated act of not-murder fully redeems him and he's subsequently shipped back to Africa for a corny, pandering happy ending that I hereby declare total bullshit. This isn't E. fucking T. or Gizmo the gremlin or that little robot from *Heartbeeps*, beloved non-human characters whose adventures taught us the power of friendship and that animals will blow up in the microwave. Hell, he isn't even Air Bud, who at least won The Big Game. (I assume. I've never seen an *Air Bud* movie, because I have a soul.) He's just a big, stupid, smelly ape that kills people. Fuck Mighty Joe

Young. The *second* that baby was safe they should've put him down with a bazooka. Put Mighty Joe Young down with the bazooka, I mean. Not the baby.

The Mighty Peking Man

(1977)

Directed by Ho Meng-Hua

There was a peeking man prowling around our neighborhood for a while, but they finally caught me. I am legally obligated to provide you with this information if you live in zip code 33629.

These cats catch wind of a gigantic, Godzilla-sized ape that's been raising hell in some backwater, so they decide to catch it. Says one: "I know a hunter here in Hong Kong, an explorer; he just lost his girl and he wants to get away. I guarantee he'd be the right man for us if he'd go." Well he would and they do, but as it turns out their expedition is a total fiasco: one joker gets stepped on by an elephant, another one loses a leg to a tiger, and eventually everyone is dead or has run away except for our main guy. Things actually work out okay for him though: not only does he locate the giant ape, but the ape's BFF – your stereotypical blonde jungle goddess – falls for him hard, and before you know it she's running through the jungle in a surreal slow-motion montage while a terrible 1970s love song plays. It's like she's in a deranged tampon commercial that, for reasons only the marketing department fully understands, involves a giant monkey and a woman swinging a doped-up cheetah around by its front legs. Eventually the lovers decide to go to Hong Kong, and since neither one of them has ever seen a movie before, they take the giant monkey too. ("Wherever we go we bring the monkey with us!") Once there the whole thing bogs down in some soap opera bullshit for a while, but eventually this joker tries to rape Jungle Girl so Mighty Peking Man goes absolutely bananas (I'm sorry; it's such an easy joke) and starts trashing toy cars and buildings, to surprisingly mixed reactions:

BYSTANDER: "What's wrong?"

PANICKED IDIOT: "There's a gorilla! A giant gorilla!"

BYSTANDER: "My wife is a gorilla too!"

Never let apocalyptic destruction and/or your impending doom prevent you from making a hackneyed "wife" joke. Naturally it all wraps up *King Kong* style with M.P.M. on top of a skyscraper, holding the blonde in one hand and his dick in the other. Ha! I'm kidding - he's fighting helicopters with the other hand. The big difference this time is that the soldiers and airmen called in to deal with *this* giant ape go out of their way to make sure they kill the girl too. I'm not really sure what *that's* all about, but the part where the giant monkey falls off one building and through the roof of another, while on fire, is nothing short of epic, so if that's what it takes to get us to such a kickass finale then as far as I'm concerned they can kill anyone they want.

Monkey Shines

(1988)

Directed by George A. Romero

I am so glad a lurid horror movie snagged this title before some awful, family-friendly monkey comedy had the chance to use it. Fuck you, families.

We open with our main guy, up at dawn and jogging down the street while wearing a backpack full of bricks. Overachieving asshole; I hope he gets hit by a... oops! Ha ha! Excellent.

So now he has something in common with my dad's old stereo setup: they're both quads! Ha ha! Confined to a wheelchair, what he really needs now is a helper hooker. There is no such thing though (I've checked), so he settles for the next best option - a helper monkey. But this is a horror movie, not some feel-good overcoming-the-odds on the other side of the mountain hanky-fest, so naturally there's a gruesome catch: unbeknownst to him, the former lab monkey that takes the job has been subsisting on a diet of human brains. Hey, it's a George Romero movie; we all knew that brains would be eaten at some point. (Aside to the guy who, right now, is saying "Excuse me, but George Romero's zombies don't eat brains! That's an entirely different movie!": This is why you don't have a girlfriend.)

So the monkey is a godsend at first: doing chores, dialing the phone, and probably jerking our main guy off in a deleted scene I'm sure exists somewhere. But then the monkey starts killing people that the main guy doesn't like, and, fully aware of this due to their ESP link (Why does he have an ESP link with the monkey? Trust me, there is no good reason.), he gives the monkey up, only to have it return like a spurned lover and run wild in his house with a straight razor. Now, a way better direction to go at this point would be for it to turn out that the main guy's paralysis was, whaddya call it, *psychosomatic* (this is actually hinted at at one point), and it was really him killing everyone and then imagining that he was seeing it through the eyes of his ESP monkey proxy. But nope, this movie is committed to killer psychic monkey, and it plays that absurd hand to the bitter end, where our main guy grabs the monkey (an obvious puppet) in his mouth and hilariously shakes it to death. I can't remember the last time I laughed so hard. It would be the dumbest horror movie scene of 1988 if it weren't for the "reverse monkey chest-burster" dream a few seconds later. Unbelievable. I swear, if I had known how this one would pan out, I never would've wasted those shrooms on *Mammoth*.

The Monkey's Paw

(2013)

Directed by Brett Simmons

From the day we're born people are encouraging us to make wishes. "Make a wish and blow out the candles!" "Wish upon a star!" "You're gonna wish you never fucked with my sister!" Yet in stories and movies wishes always backfire with hilariously ironic and/or tragic results. The most famous of these stories, of course, concerns a literal monkey's paw, a magical wishing charm which is kind of like a lucky rabbit's foot, except way luckier. At least for the rabbit. In this variation on the story, the monkey's paw (which never does flips anyone off, a wasted opportunity if I ever saw one) falls into the hands of yet another hopeless idiot, who proceeds to squander his wishes on easily-perverted pap like a new car (he immediately crashes it), bringing his dead buddy back to life (the buddy returns as a soulless monster à la the main guy in Wes Craven's *Chiller* or your ex-wife), and, the standard third wish, that age-old ninth-inning cop-out, a wish undoing the previous wishes in the hopes of putting things back to normal, even though "normal" clearly sucked or there wouldn't have been so much impetus to make all these wishes in the first place. The problem with the jerkaholics in these stories is clearly a lack of imagination. So, in order to illustrate one way to game the capricious, sarcastic wishing gods, let me tell you what *I* would wish for:

1. Infinity more wishes. (Yes, I realize that all infinity of them will horribly backfire. I'm a masochist, okay?)
2. A bucket of pussy. (I'll let you figure out what this means.) (This one will probably backfire in a particularly horrible fashion, BTW.)
3. A Kimber Riddle/Ke$ha/me threesome.
4. The *Star Wars* prequels - never happened.
5. An 8-inch penis. (The one I'm currently packing is way too big.)
6. A Kimber Riddle/Taylor Swift/me threesome.
7. Resurrect Taylor Swift after Ke$ha murders her in a jealous rage.
8. Undo the zombie apocalypse brought about by Zombie Taylor Swift. (Unintended side result: fast zombies are now known as "Swifties".)
9. Everyone is cured of cancer except for Seth MacFarlane. He gets it.
10. Avril Lavigne is now identical twins.
11. Avril Lavigne/me threesome.
12. After too many zany misunderstandings, identify once and for all which Avril is the evil twin, and which is the good one.
13. Disintegrate Good Avril.
14. Kimber Riddle/Ke$ha/Zombie Taylor Swift /Evil Avril Lavigne foursome.
15. Exclusive film rights to #14.

And that is how you manage that. You're welcome.

Mystery on Monster Island

(1981)

Directed by J. Piquer Simon

Getting married is great. There's a huge party, all your friends and family show up, everyone gets trashed, and at the end of the night you're all but guaranteed to get laid. The only downside: afterwards you have to *be* married, which tends to consist of less partying and fucking, and more compromising, arguing, and gaslighting. Our main guy has clearly figured this out, so in order to postpone his engagement he convinces his uncle, Grand Moff Tarkin, to send him on a long ocean voyage to see the world. It's a sound delaying tactic, but it all goes to shit when the boat is overrun by these wild-looking, pyromaniac fish men and subsequently explodes. Our main guy and his tutor manage to escape overboard, washing up on an unidentified island where they quickly steal everything they need from someone else's campsite, including a semi-tame chimpanzee that immediately begins engaging in hilarious slapstick, like almost killing the tutor with a loaded gun. (Guns are funny, kids! Is there maybe a gun in the house that you could be playing with right now?) Needless to say, this flick has taken a seriously dip in quality since the fish men, and the thoroughly ridiculous dinosaur that shows up next certainly doesn't help matters any. Rounding out this movie's Random Encounter Table: cannibals, shambling mounds, Bedouins, and Mothra.

In addition to playing out like an evening of Dungeons & Dragons that has gone on entirely too long, this movie fails in myriad other ways: the tutor is annoying as fuck, endlessly shrieking like an untethered bitch and contributing nothing to the cause (survival) except slapstick antics; the fights lean towards corny, *Swiss Family Robinson* type horseshit; the main bad guy looks like Spalding Gray (don't get me wrong, I like Spalding Gray, but this is very distracting); and, surprisingly late in the game, they introduce that most infuriating of tired, sub-comedic tropes, the "funny" parrot. (I am however happy to report that this parrot is on the receiving end of no small amount of abuse. At one point the bad guys shoot its tail feathers off, and later, when it cracks wise, one of them angrily knocks it off its perch. That's right: fuck you, parrot.) Worst of all, it's ultimately revealed that (most of) this wild adventure was just a hoax, dreamed up by the main guy's Uncle Tarkin and perpetrated by actors! What about the dinosaur, and the giant caterpillars? Why, they were simply giant, clockwork models! (If you ask me, this reeks more of a last-minute attempt to excuse their cheesiness, rather than a legitimate plot twist.) By extension, of course, this means that this entire movie has been a pointless, inconsequential hoax, except this time on us. Thanks for watching! Fuck you!

New Monkees

(1987)

Produced by committee

New Monkees don't need no leading article, man. Calling them *The* New Monkees would just dilute their power.

The time is the mid-1980s, and while everything is ridiculous, at least it's entertaining. (Davy) Jonesing for cheap programming, MTV decides to start airing the old *Monkees* TV show from the sixties, and apparently enough time had passed for it to get popular all over again. Everyone agreed that there had to be a way to exploit this further without sharing any of the money with the actual Monkees, so they finally decided to create a new set of Monkees called, brilliantly, the "New Monkees". They needed a band that was quintessentially 1980s; consisted of four cute, non-threatening guys; and that only occasionally recorded songs about beating your girlfriend or bedding underage chicks. Fortunately this band totally existed: they were called The Elvis Brothers, and as luck (not theirs) would have it they'd just been cut loose by their record label. The corporations involved offered them a deal: a new recording contract, plus their own syndicated TV show. All they had to do was change their name to "New Monkees". The Elvis Brothers, desperate, adrift, and unsure of their future, still told them to fuck off, so they just held auditions and picked four nobodies for the gig. The audition process alone was pretty big news at the time, but strangely enough almost nobody in the appropriate age bracket will admit that they remember any of this ever happening. Seriously, ask any ten people on your favorite social media site right now about the New Monkees and maybe *one* of them will concede that they have any idea what you're talking about. The rest will ignore you entirely, because they're busy being blandly outraged about something.

Of course, one could argue that the New Monkees non-phenom is better off forgotten since the whole thing was an unmitigated disaster from day one. The kids they picked were legitimately charismatic and funny (well, except for Marty), but original Monkees fans, showing their true sociopathic colors, flipped the fuck out and even went so far as to send death threats to the individual members, as if terrorizing some innocent, star-struck kids would somehow restore the honor of a band that was entirely manufactured to begin with. As for the show itself, well, as revisionist as I like to be even I have to admit that it was pretty fucking terrible. The gimmick was that the New Monkees lived in this gigantic unexplored mansion full of secret rooms, where anything, literally anything, could happen. I guess they were trying to combine the innocent charm of *The Monkees 1.0* with the surreal comedy of *The Young Ones* (reruns of both shows were super popular on MTV at the time, and as late as 1991 MTV was still considered moderately relevant), but it doesn't work because when literally ANYTHING can happen it's hard to care what ultimately does, so despite the occasional funny bit episodes tended to deteriorate into an deranged morass of incomprehensible idiocy, kind of like your social life but with more catchy musical interludes. Their sole album was excellent though, so Larry, Jared, Marty, Dino... if you ever read this I want you to know that I for one appreciated the effort. Even if they did end up shipping the entire run directly from the manufacturing plant to the cut-out bins.

Night of the Bloody Apes

(1971)

Directed by Rene Cardona

This doctor's son has leukemia, so he has no choice: he *has* to transplant a gorilla's heart into the son's body. (Assisting the doctor: his weird, limping assistant, who refers to him as "Master". Because why be a mad doctor if you can't be the most tiresome mad doctor stereotype imaginable?) And it's a good thing this movie is Mexican, because the AMA would certainly condemn what happens next: the son's face rapidly monkeyfies (it's a word now) and he goes completely insane. "I was prepared for everything, but not for this," the doctor says. Our crazy ape man sporadically escapes to murder people and rape chicks, while his frustrated dad drives around in a green station wagon looking for him. When one police detective guesses the truth, the doctor haughtily dismisses him by claiming that he's seen too many "pictures of terror." *Night of the Bloody Apes* is a hopeless failure as a horror movie/picture of terror, but with just a little retooling I think it would make a great sitcom. Every week the son could ape out and have a slapstick adventure, the detective hot on his trail but never quite catching him in the act, while the put-upon dad does a Ted Knight-style slow burn and his wacky, precocious assistant makes wisecracks.

Okay, maybe not.

A Nymphoid Barbarian in Dinosaur Hell

(1990)

Directed by Brett Piper

Troma Entertainment, the company that released this flick, basically invented making movies bad on purpose, with a sideline of picking up other people's bad movies and rebranding them with infuriatingly self-aware titles, because they're soulless scumholes dedicated to wiping their asses with everything they touch, and then making us smell it. So going into this one I was already slightly pissed, and thanks to her overwrought narration I instantly hated the main chick in spite of her assurances that she was a total whore, something I generally respect in women. The setting is a post-nuke Earth crawling with dinosaurs (placing creatures from the distant past in your distant future may seem counter-intuitive, but claiming your movie about a monster-infested wasteland is set in the future is always a good save in case any power lines are visible in the background of a shot, or one of your idiot actors forgets to take off his Swatch), where our unimpressive main chick is repeatedly kidnapped by a Renaissance faire reject and his pet lizard men and then rescued by her ineffectual boyfriend and/or Weequay from *Return of the Jedi*. This endless squabbling over mediocre pussy is just as boring as you'd expect, and it makes up the bulk of this awful, awful movie. That said, the mutant dinosaurs are pretty impressive – unique and well-realized via old-school special effects – but it's not worth wading through the rest of this dung pit just to see them. Besides, every time someone so much as acknowledges *A Nymphoid Barbarian in Dinosaur Hell* they're actively encouraging Troma to churn out more shitty, unwatchable garbage that succeeds solely because its mere existence makes for an easy "WTF?" post on Facebook. Me, I demand more from my trashy entertainment than half-baked toilet-scrapings sporting a click-bait title. Fuck you, Troma. When everyone on your payroll goes to Hell (and they will) they should be forced to watch nothing but the Toxic Avenger cartoon, over and over again, for eternity.

100 Million BC

(2008)

Directed by Louie Myman

It all starts when two archaeologists discover a T. rex skull and a drawing of Devil Dinosaur in a cave in Argentina. Like most things this leads to a meeting, where the dad from *Family Ties* spins a crazy yarn involving time travel and the Philadelphia Experiment (or, as we knew it back then, "Project Fiasco"). It's all a prelude to his current proposal, which is to send some soldiers back to the ~~Cretinous Croesus Creationist~~ Dinosaur Era to locate a previous team that has been stranded there since the last time they tried this. And this mission is eventually accomplished, although the rescue team does lose a few people along the way: one of them buys it instantly when he materializes in the wrong place at the right time and fuses with a tree, and naturally a few get picked off by dinosaurs. (I was especially relieved when they got the lieutenant; this gung-homo faggot calls his men "ladies" so many times that it's obvious he can barely control himself. If he hadn't been eaten by a dinosaur I guarantee this movie would've contained at least one male-on-male rape.) Now, up to this point *100 Million BC* has been a pretty good flick. It's clever and intelligent, they ask and answer all the right questions, and there's even one legitimately hilarious bit where they show one of the guys who's been stranded in the prehistoric past making a crude cave painting of a

UFO. "Just messin' around," he explains. Unfortunately, it completely falls apart once everyone returns to regular times. See, they fail to prevent this T. rex from coming through the time warp after them, and it easily busts out of the abandoned warehouse the Navy inexplicably operates its time travel out of and goes on a rampage. Don't get me wrong, this would be a perfectly fine thrilling climax if their budget allowed for a dinosaur rampaging through the city, but it obviously didn't so the end result is pretty embarrassing. And I know that movie heroes always feel the need to see shit through to the bitter end, but I still found it pretty hard to swallow when our time travel survivors decided to go after this displaced T. rex themselves. I mean seriously, they managed to survive for *years* in actual dinosaur times and now that they're finally safe they go out of their way to put themselves in the path of the only dinosaur left in the entire world? Fuck that jazz, let the cops handle it. Maybe it'll give them something useful to do instead of busting me for *one lousy joint*.

One Million Years B.C.

(1966)

Directed by Don Chaffey

This dull-as-dickwater flick often gets a pass from older movie critics because 1960s sex symbol Raquel Welch is it in, and she was quite overrated in her day. She never gets naked though so really, have some scruples, older movie critics. The story itself is so simplistic that it's barely worth reviewing. A caveman is thrown out of his tribe. He steals a girl from a rival, Aryan tribe, which is portrayed as being superior in every way because this movie is racist. Then he returns to the first tribe, where there's a cavegirl catfight that is indisputably the high point of the movie. Then the Aryans show up and everyone fights until the volcano erupts, traditionally signaling the end of your caveman/dinosaur/Pompeii movie. Honestly, why do movie cavemen always build their villages so close to active volcanos? That's what I want to know.

One of Our Dinosaurs Is Missing

(1975)

Directed by Robert Stevenson

Before the brilliant quinfecta of *The Black Hole* (1979), *The Watcher in the Woods* (1980), *Dragonslayer* (1981), *Something Wicked This Way Comes* (1983), and *Return to Oz* (1985) (*Tron*? fuck *Tron*), the long-accepted truism was that animated Disney movies were reliable, consistent instant classics, whereas live-action Disney movies were generally steaming piles of street ass. Their live-action premises were usually dumb as fuck (a lawyer that keeps turning into a sheepdog; people returning *from* Witch Mountain after they just went through tons of grief to escape *to* there; *Tron*), the plots hinged almost entirely on falling down, and the actresses never showed us their tits, like it would hurt kids *so much* if they saw a solid pair of tits once in a while. True to form, this live-action Disney movie begins when (Ah, so!) Ancient Chinese Secret is stolen by a slapsticky corporate spy, transferred to microfilm, and stashed somewhere inside a dinosaur skeleton at the museum. The spy only manages to tell one person where the microfilm is hidden before he's captured: his former nanny, who rounds up a whole mammary of nannies (it's a pride of lions, a pod of whales, and a mammary of nannies) to look for it. Later, the Chinese return to the museum, kung fu the hell out of the place, and load the entire dinosaur onto a flatbed truck, only to have the nannies steal the truck and drive it all over London, instigating slapstick havoc while being chased by, well, everybody. Yeah, it's one of *those* movies. And as you probably guessed, it all ends with a huge nanny/kung fu brawl. It's boring, it's stupid, it's full of racist stereotypes (a favorite of old-school Disney), and let me tell you, it is legitimately painful to watch the scene where the nannies all march through the museum in single file, eager to begin their mission, because you can tell that the people who made this terrible, terrible movie thought that this sequence was just bust-a-gut hilarious. Potentially iconic, even. When someone is that divorced from reality, you really can't help but feel sorry for them.

On the Comet

(1970)

Directed by Karel Zeman

This huge comet appears in the sky and just keeps getting bigger, and bigger... None of the dipshits we meet at the beginning of this movie is particularly concerned though. The main dude is especially dismissive: "It's probably just another planet, heading for us at a fantastic speed," he shrugs. Well, they should have ducked & covered, because the bastard crashes into us, a huge chunk of Earth is torn off *Space 1999* style, and a whole bunch of squabbling French soldiers and A-rabs end up stranded on the comet as it hurtles off into outer space. And because things are never so bad that they can't get worse, the place is sick with dinosaurs that start attacking the frogs' fort. Guns prove to be useless against the dinosaurs, but the frogs do mange to scare them off by crafting noisemakers out of pots and pans. Then, since they don't need them at that exact moment, they decide to throw all their guns *down a well*. Brilliant. You're not hungry right now either, so why don't you throw all your food down there too? And the dune coons still have *their* guns, so now the frogs are screwed. Leave it to the fucking French, right? Most of the special effects look like the the cartoon interludes from *Monty Python*, there's no gore, and none of the chicks get naked, but this movie is so goddamned weird that it's actually worth watching anyway.

There's a walking fish that evolves into a pig in just a few seconds, an old-timey boat sporting smokestacks that turn into cannons, puppet dinosaurs, and tons of other wild, fucked-up shit. My only real criticism is with the very end, where it turns out that the whole thing was just a dream. We've already discussed how unacceptable this cop-out was when they used it back in the nineteen teens (see *The Ghost of Slumber Mountain*, above); breaking it out in fucking *1970* is just beyond the pale. Seriously, producers of *On the Comet*, get your shit together.

The People that Time Forgot

(1977)

Directed by Kevin Connor

The worst thing about this sequel to *The Land That Time Forgot* is that it adopts the weird template introduced by *Beneath the Planet of the Apes* wherein the sequel is all about finding the missing hero of the previous movie, but as soon as they find him, he's killed. How fucking irritating is that? And at least the *Apes* guy went down hard, taking the entire fucking planet with him. This fool is finished off via an arrow fired by "Tribesman #16" or some shit. Seriously, if the Star Warriors had rescued Han Solo from Jabba the Hutt only to have a random alien fatally shoot him two minutes later, people would have been rioting in the streets. If you're just here to waste my time, movie, then maybe *you* should be paying *me* for the privilege of watching this shit. Another glaring flaw is that the main chick from Part 1, played by righteous superbabe Susan Penhaligon, doesn't return, having reportedly been hurled into a live volcano between movies, I guess because it was the only thing around that had any chance of being hotter than her. Instead, main chick duties are now handled by none other than Ursa, the evil Kryptonian bitch from *Superman II*. Don't get me wrong, find me a Kryptonite condom and I'd happily violate her

Phantom Zone, but facts are facts and my opinion is also a fact and I say she falls considerably short of her predecessor. Also, did they really need to include a cavegirl with perfect hair and teeth, who clearly Nairs her legs? I'm sorry, but that is such a 1960s approach to this type of thing.

Once we get past all the narrative and casting blunders (John Wayne's kid as the main guy? You'd be better off casting a park bench.) there are a few things to like. For starters, there's minimal dicking around: eight minutes in and our main crew is already over the Land that [Noun] Forgot, getting attacked by their first dinosaur. (Excuse me, *flying reptile*. Happy, eggheads? Fuck off.) A pterodactyl sticks its beak into an active airplane propeller. One guy dutifully keeps track of all the pterodactyls he's shot, which I found fairly funny. And the chased-back-to-the-plane climax is pretty good and was clearly the inspiration for the opening scene in *Raiders of the Lost Ark*. The dinosaurs themselves are just as cool as they were in Part 1 and there are quite a few of them in the first half, although the second half mostly finds our heroes matching dicks with a bunch of *Shogun*-looking fucks in their ridiculous "Mountain of Skulls", a low-rent Temple of Doom that looks like it was sketched by an intern the night before. (The bad guys' leader, incidentally, looks like a green Marlon Brando circa *Apocalypse Now*. And he doesn't speak English, making him nearly as incomprehensible, except without the obvious excuse of actually being Marlon Brando.) Overall, it's pretty disappointing, if not a total waste of time. I hate to admit it, but given the drastic drop in quality between Parts 1 and

2, maybe it was for the best that they never got around to filming *Out of Time's Abyss*, the third (and final) book in the "...that Time Forgot" series. We'd probably be referring to it today as "Out of Time's Anus".

Planet of Dinosaurs

(1977)

Directed by James K. Shea

From the awesome opening credits featuring ghostly dinosaurs superimposed over a starfield you know this movie is gonna rock, and it doesn't fail to disappoint. Wait, I mean is *does* fail to disappoint. The title says it all: a spaceship blows up, stranding the survivors on the nearest planet, which just happens to be inhabited by dinosaurs. And the dinosaurs in question are fucking awesome; they're so good, in fact, that the dinosaur footage from this flick has been stolen/borrowed for use in countless inferior movies. I kid you not, I've even seen it show up in *porn*. Tragically, the first person to be eaten by one of these dinosaurs is previously-unsung cinematic hottie Mary Appleseth, who, after stripping down to her bra and panties (thank you thank you thank you) takes an ill-advised swim and is gobbled up. I'm not exaggerating when I say that this might be the most egregious example of HCDF (Hottest Chick Dies First) Syndrome I've ever seen. I understand that sometimes the hottest chick has to go first simply because she's the worst actor in the bunch, but there's no way in this or any other hell that our girl was any worse than fellow castaways Buff McMoustache or Miss Midriff McGee, whose lines really should've been limited to "Oh, God, it's eating me!" (Or, in Miss Midriff's case, "Oh, God! Fuck me!"). Oh, and by

"Buff McMoustache" I'm referring to the blonde guy. Sorry I wasn't more specific. I forgot that this movie was made in the 1970s. Shitty acting aside, this is inarguably one of the best dinosaur movies ever made. It's got beautiful women, great monsters, a simple but serviceable story, a nice scuzzy 1970s vibe, and even a smidgen of gore. Why it isn't widely recognized as a B-movie classic is a complete mystery, and why it didn't tear up the fucking box office when it was originally released is, like, a *double* mystery. What other notable sci-fi movies even came out in 1977?

Planet of the Apes

(1968)

Directed by Franklin J. Schaffner

It's easy to forget how long it took the very first *Planet of the Apes* movie to get to the big reveal, which is pretty ridiculous seeing as it's given away right in the title. Instead, we open with our main guy, one of four astronauts on a deep-space mission, endlessly blathering on and on to no one in particular, wallowing in his own hubris like a pig in shit. "Captain's Log, Stardate 2673, I'm a pretentious butthole, blah blah blah..." Even their subsequent crashdown on a mysterious planet isn't enough to shut this guy up; he just keeps running at the mouth without missing a beat. In fact, he gives one of his fellow astronauts so much unwarranted shit that I'm surprised the guy doesn't pop him in the fucking snout right then and there. What an ass. So anyway, this might be a good time to go make a sandwich or call your girlfriend back or even take a nap, because our marooned astronauts spend the next *twenty minutes* just trudging through the desert. Okay, desert, we got it. Now fucking *do* something. Finally they locate some fellow humans, but then, suddenly, they're all attacked by talking, rifle-wielding apes! And again, this would be a real shocker *if the goddamned movie wasn't called "Planet of the Apes"*. Now if you were watching a romantic comedy or something and all of a sudden a bunch of gun-toting apes came rolling in and started capping the shit out of everyone, *that* would blow your fucking mind. In fact, Hollywood should seriously consider having the Planet of the Apes apes just unexpectedly show up in an unrelated movie once every year or so. And it should be completely random, so that even the people making the movie don't know it's gonna happen until the very last second. "Guess what, cast and crew of *Before Midnight*, you're the surprise Ape movie for 2013!" God *damn* would that be entertaining. Seriously Hollywood, I know times are tough, so if you wanna put asses back in those theater seats you need to launch this program, pronto. As for the original *Planet of the Apes* here, well, for my money it's been totally eclipsed by the increasingly delirious/absurd sequels, of which there are at least four and as many as twelve, depending on how you're counting. Still, it does deliver one of the biggest twist endings of all time, so thank you, 20th Century Fox, for spoiling it on the front cover of several versions of the DVD. You stupid fucks.

Planet of the Apes

(2001)

Directed by Tim Burton

Most of the original *Planet of the Apes* adventures began with modern-day astronauts crash-landing on Planet Ape and coming up with new ideas is hard, so that's how this one starts too. This time our main astronaut is honky-hop footnote and *Wahlburgers* producer "Marky" Mark Wahlberg, and over the course of this bafflingly pointless, color-by-numbers remake he's captured by the apes, escapes, aimlessly runs around for a while, squanders multiple opportunities to mack on this insanely hot blonde who totally wants his jock, is outed as a homosexual (this is implied), and eventually convinces his fellow humans to rise up and do battle with their poop-hurling masters. So who wins? Nobody. (Certainly not us.) Instead, they wrap it all up with a *deus ex machina* (this is Latin for "complete bullshit") and man and ape learn to live in harmony for the foreseeable future i.e. until they blindside us with a nonsensical twist ending a few minutes later. It's a failure any way you look at it, but ultimately this is a movie made up entirely of missed opportunities. The all-out war at the end features zillions of men and apes kicking the absolute shit out of each other and yet there's not a single drop of blood. The hot blonde never gets naked. (The original *Planet of the Apes* was rated G and we saw the main guy's ass; this one is *PG-13* and they couldn't favor us with some tits?) They don't even add anything new or unexpected to the story, unless "so far out of left field that it doesn't make a lick of goddamned sense" counts as "unexpected", and for the purposes of making my point I'm going to say that it doesn't. The biggest missed opportunity of all though is the soundtrack, which is the same ponderous, *faux*-epic orchestral blandness that they always saddle quasi-important sci-fi movies with. How in the name of Gorilla Jesus did someone in the cross-promotional department not think to have Marky Mark record an ape-themed rap to play over the end credits? They could have billed him as "Marky Mark and the Monkey Bunch"! Too goofy, you say? For a movie that ends with a shot of monkey Abraham Lincoln? For a movie with a twist ending so incomprehensible that even nerds have given up debating it? For a movie that's so temporally illogical that it's been openly excised from the **Planet of the Apes** chronology? For real, if you think a white-boy rap about orangutans would have made this movie any dumber, you really need to adjust your barometer.

Play-Mate of the Apes

(2002)

Directed by John Bacchus

When most people find out that something particularly aberrant exists – like, say, a porno based on *Planet of the Apes* – their immediate reaction is to re-post it, add a pithy comment ("This: LOL! Because reasons. WTF?"), and hope they set their filters properly so that Grandma doesn't see it. If, however, you're the type who's tempted to investigate further, then first you **must** ask yourself one very important question:

Do I *really* want to watch a movie that will almost certainly feature a washed-up stripper having sex with a monkey?

Of course the answer is yes, but unfortunately this flick doesn't deliver. In fact, it's just a bunch of dyking out, not that this is a bad thing since the main chick is Misty Mundae (so choice). Frankly though I was hoping for something a little more far more disturbing. None of the other dames in this flick even approaches Misty's hotness level (too many of them have unnaturally huge, deformed tits), but they're all doable, with the sole exception of the blonde who ends up getting lobotomized. (Q: What do you do after you lobotomize a blonde? A: Patent your free energy machine! Ha ha! Yeah, I wrote that joke and I don't get it either.) There are some okay gags too ("And I'm gonna miss you most of all, Scarecrow."), which is pretty amazing for a script that was probably typed with one hand. What the fuck is up with the last half hour though? There's a rap and everyone dances, and later there's another song and everyone dances again... They're not even naked! That's valuable time we could have spent looking at Misty's tits. Let me give you Kansas City faggots some advice: any time you're making a movie that is not explicitly about dancing and you think "We could use some people dancing here," you are WRONG. Unless you're in Bollywood, in which case you're still wrong, but it's politically incorrect to point it out.

In an unexpected, incomprehensible move, someone actually remade this flick as a "serious" movie, *Empire of the Apes* (2013).

Poseidon Rex

(2013)

Directed by Mark L. Lester

Or P. Rex, for short. And no, you can't use that as your *new* new handle, Sean Combs. You're a goddamned idiot, you know that?

An insipid young couple whose relationship hinges entirely on witless bickering gets caught up in an undersea treasure hunt. Well, the guy does, at least. The chick, a total killjoy who's nowhere near hot enough to be such a drag, accuses him of "acting like he's in *The Goonies*" and fucks off on a party boat with some brain-damaged lunkheads instead. (These guys were perfectly cast, by the way.) So yeah, the *only* reason to keep watching this is because there's a huge aquatic dinosaur out there, and hopefully it will eat the lot of them. Don't get me wrong, I love movies where something in the water wants to eat you, and I love dinosaurs, so a killer aquatic dinosaur movie is right up my alley. One problem: despite the vast number of sea-going dinosaurs to choose from, this flick decided to go the *Sharknado* route and try to wow us with a goddamned *aquatic Tyrannosaurus rex*. To their credit though they do play the whole thing straight – eschewing the whole "awful on purpose/so bad it sucks" approach that is *way* past its expiration date – so while I wouldn't go tattooing the title on my dick or anything ultimately it's an okay monster sub-genre mash-up. I loved it when the actor playing the main kid decided to YOLO it and blatantly cops a feel while his character is giving his girl CPR, there's one solid jump-scare, and some of the characters don't end up where you'd expect them to, which is probably just a result of careless/lazy writing but has the accidental side effect of making the story a lot less predictable. And while the featured scientist chick isn't the hottest ever, and her rack is too big, she rocks a bikini to a sufficient degree and stocks cold beer in her lab, so she's definitely a keeper. Given a choice though I'd take the military chick with the freckles, who, sadly, I was unable to identify in the credits. She could put in a request for a weekend pass, I'll rent us a suite, and we can spend two solid days eating room service and boning while everyone else is out at sea, fighting the dinosaur. Now that's how you survive a monster movie in style.

Primal Force

(1999)

Directed by Nelson McCormick

Okay, would you return to the killer baboon-infested island where you once almost died just to rescue a lawyer and a cute, snotty teenage girl? Yeah, I'd probably go in for the girl too. But she'd better put out afterwards. If you've read this far I'm sure you can guess what happens next, which puts you ahead of most of the characters, at least. See, for reasons known only to the writer, the main guy obstinately refuses to share important information with the rest of his group until they're ass-deep in monkey territory, preferring to endlessly shake his dick at their party's beta male instead. In a smarter movie this would be gloriously ironic, but trust me, this is not a smarter movie. Still, it's a fun flick, and it actually makes an effort across the board instead of throwing all of its eggs into one aspect (like, say the cartoon effects) and failing anyway. So yeah, not too shabby for a killer monkey movie. I have to admit, I'm kind of disappointed. I had a great bit about it being a primal *farce*.

Pterodactyl

(2005)

Directed by Mark L. Lester

Usually the first clue that monsters are creeping around is when someone finds a giant tooth, or a giant footprint, or the black guy's body. In this movie the first clue is when they discover some giant piss. Which of course begs the question, how does one differentiate giant piss from, well, just a whole lot of regular piss? I guess that's why I'm not a scientist. Anyway, when the pterodactyls get done peeing they decide to carry everyone off for dinner, and I guess a couple of them are wielding machetes too because somehow during their frequent fly-bys they're effortlessly cutting people's heads off. It looks like the pterodactyls are holding all the cards (I assume in the claw that isn't holding the machete) until some army dudes show up to blast those flying freaks to fuck and back. All told, it's not the worst movie ever made: it's pretty gory, the blonde who strips down to her underwear for a swim is a solid piece of ass, and the cartoon pterodactyls only look like crap about half the time. There could have been a lot more tits popping out while everything was going down, but I was thinking the same thing regarding the checkout line at Target today, so I guess that goes without saying.

Raptor

(2001)

Directed by Jay Andrews

A dinosaur escapes from this secret lab and one of the first people it attacks is the sheriff's daughter (after we see her tits, fortunately). She survives, but now she's in shock, not that her halfwit dad really gets this:

DOCTOR: "I'm afraid your daughter is suffering from a rare form of traumatic catalepsy."

SHERIFF: "And that would be what, doctor?"

DOCTOR: "Well, something so terrified your girl that she shut off part of her mind to avoid thinking about it."

SHERIFF: "That's not like her."

Later the sheriff and a chick with the largest rack money can buy investigate the lab and are trapped inside. Fortunately for them the government (ours) is on the case and sends in several distinct commando units to save the day, including a team wearing berets, a team decked out in raincoats, and a team sporting winter camouflage, even though this crisis is occurring in the American Southwest. And indoors. Since his jig, whatever it was, is obviously up, the bad guy frees all his dinosaurs and they start killing everybody (at least one of these kills is recycled from *Carnosaur 2*) until finally our mix & match military strike force (seriously, the G.I. Joe team had more consistent uniforms) blows the entire lab to kingdom crap. The dinos gorily eviscerate a few people along the way and the sheriff's daughter does have a nice pair, but this is one of those movies that doesn't go quite far enough. In a better monster movie a lot more people would've been gruesomely dismembered, for example, and why the hell did our main actress invest in a rack that can probably be seen from space if she isn't gonna show those puppies off? Jesus saline-leaking Christ, get with the program you clueless, shallow bimbo.

Raptor Island

(2004)

Directed by Stanley Isaacs

Holy fucking shit, the plane at the beginning of this movie is so blatantly, unapologetically fake that I was sure they were building up to a cute little fake-out, like it would turn out to be a toy plane hanging in the cockpit of the actual plane or something. But nope, it represents a real fucking plane, which quickly crashes. This is gonna be hilarious.

Forty years later the U.S.S. *Drake* (it can't rap) has tracked some terrorists to the same general vicinity, and once everyone we're concerned with (well, in theory) ends up on the island where the toy plane crashed it's every awful Syphilis Channel/dinosaur movie cliché you've ever seen and I think they even invented some new ones. We've got cartoon monsters, people endlessly wandering around in the woods, Lorenzo Lame-ass in a starring role, radiation as a contributing factor (apparently these dinosaurs are also "mutants", although what, exactly, that means in this case is never made entirely clear), and there's even a volcano that's just jonesing to erupt. It all adds up to one big fat zero though, and the end result is so generic that it should come in a plain white box with "Dinosaur Action Movie" stenciled on the front.

And when you open it, there's a dried-up dog turd inside.

Raptor Ranch

(2013)

Directed by Dan Bishop

Several unlikable douchebags descend on the same small town, home to still more unlikable douchebags. In all we're saddled with two standard-issue college fucks, a fat metalhead/loser, a gay black pimp, a dumb blonde, and a goth chick who'd be hella cute if she'd just stop sneering for two seconds. (I can hear the director now: "Okay, you're goth, so, I dunno, sneer a lot. Oh, and you're on drugs because, you know, 'the scene.'") Also on hand: two FBI agents, one played by Lorenzo Lame-ass, who seems to be carving an entire second career out of appearing in terrible raptor movies. For typically dumb reasons everyone ends up at the local mad scientist's farm, where he just happens to keep his dinosaurs. "Doors? I love the Doors!" says the metalhead when he sees a circuit breaker labeled "Doors", so he immediately flips the switch and sets all the dinosaurs free. (There's also a breaker labeled "Beth", the name of the biggest dinosaur. The metalhead flips that one too, I guess because he also loves Peter Criss.) The story is every kind of dumb and the acting is shockingly bad, even for a cast where the indisputable frontrunner is Lorenzo Lame-ass. Still, there are plenty of dinosaur attacks, and I'm never one to discount a cute goth chick. It's just barely watchable.

Return to the Lost World

(1992)

Directed by Timothy Bond

After suffering through multiple movie interpretations of *The Lost World* and not being particularly impressed by any of them, I was still curious about this sequel to the 1992 version, which came out the very same year and I'm sure wasn't rushed or anything. Free from the constraints of the original novel's storyline, maybe they'd actually do something interesting. Ha ha! I know, right? I have to say that going in though, or it'll seem like I'm not being impartial.

So, white people have inevitably arrived in the Lost World, and within minutes they're blowing things up and oppressing the black man. Everybody from the first movie agrees to come back and help, but two of our main guys are feuding so of course comedic subterfuge is required to get them both to participate, a nice way to eat up some time in the not-so-lost regular world, where it's considerably cheaper to film. All told, our heroes manage to dick around for a good 52 minutes before they even *get* to the Lost World, which at this rate will be riddled with strip malls and fast food joints before they can even agree on their next course of action. Not that I was any more impressed when they finally did get there; the "Lost World", passable enough in the first movie, now looks suspiciously like the undeveloped lot behind any given Target, and the dinosaur models look plenty shoddy too, even more so than in Part 1, which is pretty bizarre seeing as these flicks were almost certainly filmed back-to-back. Maybe in the interim somebody accidentally left them out in the rain or something. (Not that we're exposed to much dinosaur action anyway, since this is the kind of dinosaur movie that ends with a gunfight between two groups of humans. Because that's what we all tuned in to see, right?) Hell, the effects in this movie are so lazy/bad that even something as simple as a red-hot stick pulled out of a campfire looks fake. I think they just painted the tip orange. *Return to the Lost World* is clearly meant for adults (the problems are more cerebral, less "Shoot it! Shoot it!"; a guy dies horribly via fire; there's some almost-nudity), but it's too dumb even for little kids, as evidenced by the scene where a child survives being blown to pieces and having an entire mountain collapse on him, solely by virtue of the fact that this movie sucks cock.

The actor playing the reporter, meanwhile, would go on to suck even more cock as the male lead in *Will & Grace*.

Return to the Planet of the Apes

(1975)

Produced by DFE Films

One way the *Planet of the Apes* movies were different from the book is that, in the book, the apes were just as advanced as human beings were at the time, i.e. they had cars, telephones, electricity, rock music, and probably tentacle porn. They claimed that the reason they changed this for the movie is that the original concept would cost too much, which of course makes zero sense if you stop to think about it, even for just a couple of seconds. Why would it cost MORE to make a movie set in a world that's exactly like ours, except with apes? I mean, to do it their way, they had to build an entire primitive ape city, which probably cost at least as much as Charlton Heston's ego rinse. But follow the book's lead and you could shoot the thing at the goddamned mall. Obviously there was *something* shady going on. My guess: some sort of obscure tax dodge.

Anyway, this last-gasp-before-we-mothball-the-whole-concept cartoon series tries to have it both ways, so it's a weird amalgamation where the apes live in a city that's cross between ancient Jerusalem and downtown Tulsa. It's inarguably a continuation of the movies though, because characters from the movies are occasionally mentioned by name and/or show up, even though I'm pretty sure some of them, like that chick Nova, should be dead at this point. (Come to think of it, didn't the entire planet explode right after she got the dog tags from the guy in Part 2, which we see her wearing here? Whatever; it's not my job to keep track of this shit.) As befits a show being produced inside a coffin while the lid is being nailed shut, the people who made this cartoon were exceptionally cheap and lazy, so episodes are mostly talk, peppered with moments of absolute mindfuck insanity: the mutant cult from *Beneath the Planet of the Apes* appear in spiffy baby-blue robes, shooting lasers out of their faces; an ape in a pickup truck listens to an entire ape-themed country & western song; the heroes are attacked by a giant spider and a sea serpent (not at the same time); two apes discuss a movie they want to see: "The Apefather"; the apes' sole airplane inexplicably sports markings indicating how many Native American stereotypes they've shot down; there's a Tomb of the Unknown Ape, a William Apespeare, and an ape *Mona Lisa*; the big climax involves, in part, a fight between a giant ape and a flying dragon; and I spotted at least one ape, in a crowd scene, wearing a Hawaiian shirt. In its defense though, unlike most old cartoons (or most old TV shows, for that matter) it does tell one continuous story with a beginning, middle, and end. Hell, there's even character arcs and all that fancy shit. (Pro tip: it helps to watch the episodes in the correct order.) Put it all together, and I guess you could say that *Return to the Planet of the Apes* is a lot like life: kinda terrible, but thoroughly entertaining.

Rise of the Planet of the Apes

(2011)

Directed by Rupert Wyatt

When you spend any time at all thinking about it (which is more than the writers spent, obviously), the original *Planet of the Apes* timeline makes no fucking sense. I mean, for Parts 1 and 2 to occur the apes have to go back in time and make Parts 3 and 4 happen first, but how can they do that if they don't already exist in Parts 1 and 2? For it all to work, the Planet of the Apes must have originally come about in some other manner, only for its origins to have been altered later. And to its credit, this decades-later sequel (officially Part 6, arguably Part 11) actually addresses that. It's like a sci-fi nerd's complex blog entry "fixing" some issue only he cares about, but on a Hollywood budget.

So, up to now cutting-edge Alzheimer's research hasn't produced anything but killer sharks (cf. *Deep Blue Sea*, thoroughly spanked in my book *Shark Weak*), but this time it results in exceptionally intelligent monkeys, one of which is spirited off and adopted by James Franco, who was wise to take this role because his range could actually be judged impressive when playing opposite a monkey. Ha ha! *I'm kidding.* The monkey in this movie is a computer-generated cartoon, so obviously it has considerably more range than James Franco. James has out-acted several pieces of furniture in his time though, and I think I read in *The Hollywood Reporter* that he once successfully convinced a waiter that he needed more butter.

Anyway, The CG cartoon monkey is about as lovable as a series of ones and zeroes could possibly be – i.e. not at all – but I guess we're supposed to sympathize when it inevitably goes (I promise, last time) *bananas* and ends up locked in the animal shelter. Of course James Franco is furious (look closely - it's hard to tell), despite the fact that he's the (literally) criminally irresponsible asshole who's entirely to blame, and at this point he should probably be facing any number of criminal charges and lawsuits as a result. CG Monkey (this would be a great stage name, BTW), meanwhile, is bribing his fellow shelter apes into being his friend with cookies, and then injecting the lot of them with the formula that made *him* smart, samples of which he obtains from James Franco's *home refrigerator* because apparently monkeys aren't the only thing James is stealing from work and then just irresponsibly keeping around the house. (Yes, I realize that he was previously injecting his Alzheimer's-striken father with this formula, but his father has since died so at this point Franco's behavior is hovering somewhere between kleptomania and hoarding, with a dash of not being able to act.) Finally, CG Monkey raises an entire ape army (it's a pretty big animal shelter, and for some reason it specializes in apes, I guess? Christ, I dunno.) and leads them in an all-out battle with the pigs, or as "all-out" as Hollywood's usual, desperate scrambling for a PG-13 rating will allow.

I've always been underwhelmed by the Planet of the Apes movies set in the years before it actually becomes the Planet of the Apes, but unlike their first stab at explaining this shit (*Conquest of the Planet of the Apes*) at least this movie makes *some* goddamned sense. I suppose that means it's watchable, for what it is. I am baffled by their choice of James Franco though. You're telling me a cardboard cutout of Jeff Buckley wasn't available?

Sabretooth

(2002)

Directed by James D.R. Hickox

These scientists are looking for a way to clone organs for transplants and whatnot, so naturally they begin by cloning a saber-toothed tiger. I swear, when it comes to movie science there really is no concept of cause and effect at all, is there? Of course when they decide to put that pussy in a box and take it somewhere on a flatbed truck the truck crashes, allowing it to escape. Enter dumb kids on a nature hike, and from here it pretty much writes itself. Seeing as saber-toothed tigers are so goddamned cool that even National Geographic documentaries about them aren't (entirely) boring, you'd think this would be a difficult movie to screw up. The producers of *Sabretooth* found a way though by utilizing the classic bad monster movie trifuckta: minimal gore, no tits, and too many cartoon effects. The only good thing about this flick: Nicole Tubiola as the girl in the "Hottie" t-shirt. (Truth in advertising, baby. Proper.) This would have been an infinitely better movie if it had been about *her* pussy.

Sands of the Kalahari

(1965)

Directed by Cy Endfield

A plane crashes after flying into a swarm of locusts, stranding the survivors in the desert. They manage to find food and water soon enough, but one asshole elects himself royal cock of the walk and starts eliminating the competition so as to claim all the supplies – and the sole piece of ass – for himself. And it should come as no surprise that he also utterly refuses to wear a shirt. In fact, early on he forces his shirt on the guy they send for help – even though this guy insists he doesn't need it – solely as an excuse, I'd wager, to prance around bare-chested for the foreseeable future. I'll bet you've encountered insecure dorks like this. They generally attend a lot of live sporting events. Our main asshole culls the herd by running them off into the desert one by one and then telling the others that they decided to go for help, or to the store or something ("Obviously I can't go! I don't even have a shirt!"), although one oldster, a former Nazi, doesn't go for it and he's forced to literally beat this fool to death. (Trust me, whatever your beliefs, this is one time you'll be rooting for the Nazi.) The simpering main chick backs up the asshole throughout, her lust for cock repeatedly trumping other people's lives, but eventually she does turn on him and just in time because they're rescued shortly thereafter, putting her right back on the winning team and seriously can someone please strangle this bottomless cooze? Knowing that he may encounter some inconvenient legal hassles should he return to civilization, the asshole opts to stay behind, only to be brutally slaughtered by the baboons he's been antagonizing for the bulk of the movie. Obviously there's minimal monkey action in this one, but it's entertaining enough. It would've been a lot more satisfying if the baboons had also killed the main chick though. Fuck that opportunistic bitch.

Sliders "In Dinos Veritas"

(1996)

Written by Steven Brown

Sliders was a show with a great premise, a decent cast (even the insufferable John Rhys-Davies comports himself well here, by which I mean you almost never want to punch him in the face), and a particularly delectable main chick. So naturally the Fox Network began interfering with it almost immediately, first showing the episodes out of order, then forcing them to drop some of the cooler secondary characters and themes, and finally turning it into a complete joke that relied almost entirely on novelty and full-frontal female nudity and I wish I wasn't lying about the nudity. It still occasionally managed to be kinda good, but the magic was gone, and I think it's safe to say that it began its final slide (heh) into "gimmick of the week" territory with this episode – obviously inspired by a then-recent blockbuster movie – featuring an alternate Earth where cartoon dinosaurs aren't entirely extinct and are contained in a gigantic natural preserve. A Jurassic park, if you will. Truthfully it's not that bad of an episode, but it was everything *Sliders* initially promised not to be, and it really was the beginning of a slow, agonizing decline full of compromises, dumb twists, and goofy, inane shit, stretched out over the three subsequent seasons this show managed to stay on the air.

I guess what I'm saying here is, *Firefly* fans, count your blessings.

A Sound of Thunder

(2005)

Directed by Peter Hyams

This movie is about a company that offers time travel services to the public. Think about that for a minute. I mean *really* think about it. Just imagine all the awesome fucking shit you could do if you had access to consumer-grade time travel:

- You could look up legendary pieces of historic ass like Cleopatra, Helen of Troy, and Sunny Johnson and bang the shit out of them.
- You could track down the great-great-great-grandparents of people you don't like and offer to trade them amazing future technology (like a laser pointer, or one of those novelty drinking birds) if they'll get an abortion.
- You could accuse random people of being witches.
- You could buy hundreds of rare comic books at cover price, bring them back to the present, and then tear them in half, one at a time, right in front of some nerds.
- You could crash every awesome, completely out-of-control party in history. ("Banquet of Chestnuts, this weekend! Who's in?")
- You could steal all sorts of cool, weird shit just to have it - like one of Abraham Lincoln's goofy hats,

or the dish King Tut kept his change in or whatever.

- You could make tons of bread betting on football games, horse races, presidential electrons, duels, wars, and anything else you could possibly think of:

YOU: "Double or nothing that junk scow the *Titanic* sinks within a week."

HISTORICAL MORON: "You're on, asshole."

That's just off the top of my head, and I've been taking bong hits all morning. But what do the people in this movie do? *They take tourists back in time to kill the same individual dinosaur over and over again.* That's fucking pathetic; people just don't have any imagination anymore. Also, after the first trip wouldn't they just keep bumping into the previous tour groups? Irregardless, even with this limited amount of meddling they still manage to screw up the timeline, except for some reason everyone we're (theoretically) concerned with stays the same and it's just the stuff around them that changes. (Talk about retarded. Any dipshit knows that this isn't how the entirely imaginary process of time travel works.) So what are our heroes confronted with when everything around them changes? Dinosaurs with baboon heads. I would be exaggerating if I said that this was the dumbest thing I ever saw in a major Hollywood movie, but it's definitely in the top ten. Seriously, if I wrote a bunch of animal names on slips of paper and randomly combined them by picking them out of, say, Abraham Lincoln's hat, I'd come up with something better than baboon-dinosaur, mainly because "baboon" wouldn't even be in there. There's no gore, a sex scene with no nudity, and the baboonosaurs aren't even sporting glorious, rainbow-colored baboon asses, which would've at least provided the producers with the opportunity to dub in some farting and pretend that this was *meant* to be a comedy.

Hey, I just thought of another great use for time travel: going back in time to make sure *A Sound of Thunder* never gets made.

Steel Justice

(1992)

Directed by Christopher Crowe

If you assumed that this was an awful, failed comic book from the 1990s you'd only be two-thirds right. It's actually a TV show, with a premise so ridiculous that it puts the "high" back in "high concept". See, there's this cop whose kid died via hilarious overkill during a rocket-launcher drive-by, and one day, for no comprehensible reason, a magical time traveler appears and teaches the cop that by utilizing "an underused portion of your brain" (a concept the producers are no doubt familiar with) he can turn one of his dead son's toys into a gigantic, robot dinosaur. Or, more specifically, he changes the toy into real-life mechanical dinosaur "Robosaurus", which you may be familiar with if you're the type of person who attends a lot of monster truck rallies, and if you are that person then congratulations for actually reading a book. If blood starts coming out of one or both of your ears, seek emergency assistance immediately, by which I mean "Git help kwik!" The movie is set in a garish neon-*noir* near-future cribbed from *Highlander II*, where everything is always kind of hot and shitty, but not so hot that anyone actually dresses for it (everyone seems to be wearing an overcoat) or so shitty that they can't eventually convince some fool to finance *Highlander III*. The toy-enlivening process, meanwhile, is called "The Blossoming", which is reminiscent of "The Quickening" and has nothing to do with former child star Blossom, which is unfortunate. Me, I would have called it "The Pinocchioing". The gimmick is obviously *RoboCop* meets *Jurassic Park* (I'm sure this is *exactly* how they described it at the pitch meeting), but the end result in no way resembles either of those things; mostly it's just a parade of bewildering lunacy featuring sax-playing time travelers, evil experimental percussion groups, and an ugly, gravelly-voiced lady cop who's infuriated when a crook says to her "Lookin' *good,* baby." Seriously, toots, I'd take any compliment I could get if I were you. What really sinks *Steel Justice* though is that it's so laughably earnest, like they really thought they were making engaging television here and not an extra-long promo for the next air show that's counting on the additional draw of a car-munching robot dinosaur. Because lets face it, air shows by themselves are fucking boring, and they can't all book Eddie Money. Oh, and for those of you who are going to watch this anyway, only at the very end does the cop finally summon Robosaurus, who of course demolishes a car because that's his one and only shtick and I really don't see how they expected to develop an entire TV series around it. Then again, *The Dukes of Hazzard* ran for what, seven seasons? So what do I know?

Bonus Insanity: The legal gibberish at the end of the videotape release reminds us that it is a violation of copyright law to show this movie on oil rigs.

Supergator

(2007)

Directed by Brian Clyde

Another day, another big, fake, cartoon alligator. This ~~Sci-Fi~~ ~~Syfy~~ Syphilis Channel movie features a super tasty redhead who never gets naked and gore so fake it actually ruined my day, but the very worst part is when the alligator invades a luau. (I'm surprised they didn't play the heavy-handed irony card here and make it an alligator festival.) See, the main cats are all respected (well, one assumes) scientists who have been monitoring the local volcano, so when they beat the gator to the luau with minutes to spare all they had to do was yell "The volcano's erupting!" and everyone, trusting their volcano expertise, would've probably run for cover, sparing many lives. Instead, they insist that a giant alligator is coming so of course no one believes them and many are eaten. Didn't anyone ever tell these clowns that sometimes lies are okay if you're sparing someone's feelings or preventing them from being eaten by a prehistoric monster? It's just so goddamned moronic. Christ, how stupid/talentless/drunk does a person have to be before they won't let them write material for the Syphilis Channel? For real, it would've taken *five fucking minutes* to make this movie ten times better than it is, and five more minutes to make it ten times better than that. It's like the opposite of the law of diminishing returns, but apparently not one cockhole on the *Supergator* payroll could be bothered and now I have to waste another two hours of my life cleaning up after their perfect storm of dripping shit. I hate this movie, I hate everyone involved in its production, and I hate anyone sorry enough to have ever slept with anyone involved in its production. I don't hate anyone who ever slept with that second group though, because that would be ridiculous. I'm not herpes. Exceptions are extended to executive producer Roger Corman (he's produced so many great movies that *Supergator* only cancels out a couple of them) and the redhead (who is unquestionably a gift from the gods). As for the rest of you miserable fuck-suckers: screw you. Screw you all.

Tammy and the T-Rex

(1994)

Directed by Stewart Raffill

A movie about a dead teenager possessing a robot dinosaur, starring the greatest Bond girl of all time (Denise Richards, duh) and ironic traffic fatality Paul Walker? Oh, it exists, and even in a world that gave us *Steel Justice* (see above) *Tammy and the T-Rex* is still the most insane robot dinosaur movie ever made.

Paul Walker and some other chump get into a fight over Denise Richards, a fight that ends with them grabbing each others balls. Paul Walker wins (I guess), but later the loser and his gang of 1980s-style toughs chase him down, beat him with a baseball bat, and then abandon him in a wildlife park, where he's brutally attacked by a lion. It's comedy! Paul survives, but he's in a coma, and when this mad doctor learns that he has no surviving relatives who might object he transplants Paul's brain into a life-size anima-botic Tyrannosaurus rex, which is the kind of thing we'd better get used to now that Obamacare is firmly in place. Mad sciencing unwilling victims into something that can kill you is never a good idea, so naturally the robot dinosaur graphically chews the mad doctor's guts out at the end *and then spits them into a woman's face*. It also bites his assistant's head off (the headless body attempts to flee and makes it several feet before collapsing), crushes a dude's skull, eviscerates a guy, tears a hottie's leg off, decapitates the homo whose balls he was mutually stroking earlier, and then hottie-naps Denise Richards and plays dinosaur charades with her until she finally realizes who he is. Denise and her gay black sidekick (gay black sidekicks were an inexplicably popular 1980s' trope, suggesting how long this script was laying around before the success of *Jurassic Park* finally allowed some lunatic to actually film it) decide to jack Paul Walker's body during his funeral so they can reinstate his brain and bring him back to life, but not only is his corpse already in an advanced state of decay, the coffin is inexplicably full of *live rats*. Oh my god I would so sue that mortician. Their plan B? *They try to steal another body from the morgue to transplant the brain into,* which is even more disturbing when you remember that Denise Richards fully intends to have sex with the end result. Ultimately, our story ends the only way it could: with the mad doctor gruesomely murdered and Denise Richards doing a strip tease for a horny, disembodied brain.

I love the fact that movies like this exist. It's way too violent/ gory for little kids (especially in its original, uncut version, which I'm describing here) and way too silly/dumb for anyone else, so who in the hell was the target audience? My theory? Nobody. Nobody was the target audience. I think *Tammy and the T-Rex* is filmmaking for its own sake, produced with zero regard for critical acclaim or marketing concerns or even turning a profit. In short, it's art in its purest form, and, as such, it is glorious. My only question: Why, why, why didn't they call it "I Was a Teenage Dinosaur"?

Teenage Cavegirl

(2004)

Directed by Nicholas Medina

The time is one million years ago (exactly, I guess), and since there ain't no statutory rape laws in caveman days Teenage Cavegirl is currently taking it up the ass from just about the ugliest Willem Dafoe-looking tool I've ever seen. Welcome to porn! And I see they cast a chick with trashy modern-day tattoos as the cavegirl, although now that I think about it what other choice did they have? "Find me a chick who's trashy enough to appear in porn, but who doesn't have a tramp stamp!" is a mighty tall order, is all I'm saying. Later Teenage Cavegirl goes for a stroll and we see some terrible cartoon dinosaurs, a giant cartoon scorpion, and even a dinosaur footprint rendered via cartoon effects. Seriously, they couldn't just get down in the dirt and fabricate a passable footprint with a garden trowel or something? They had to pay the computer guy to do it? How fucking lazy can you get? Anyway, Teenage Cavegirl soon traipses through a time warp and into regular times, where she makes lots of new friends who want to fuck her. Eventually her mongoloid-looking caveman boyfriend finds his way through the time gate too, and he quickly tracks her down, crashes the party, and engages a couple of modern chicks in a threesome.

This, of course, is when my teenage ward, Brittany, decided to unexpectedly roll in.

BRITTANY: *What* are you *watching?*

ME: Caveman orgy.

BRITTANY: Can I watch?

ME: If you want. They'll probably put me in jail though.

BRITTANY [sitting down]: I'll visit you.

Now, if you're casting primarily for looks and, as a result, need to make a movie with minimal dialogue, caveman porn is definitely the way to go. The action here moves to regular times pretty quickly though, and once there it's painfully apparent that our actors are fucking *horrible*. Even for porn. Even for dinner theater. Even for your cousin's dumb improv group. The worst offender, by far, is Alexandre Boisvert, an all-time loser who, in real life, insists that people call him "Voodoo" and claims that Lindsay Lohan (among others) pays him for sex. He comports himself just as laughably here - this talentless shitmarker couldn't convey pain if he was on fire. I know it's just porn, and you're playing the guy, but either put in the effort and earn your Arby's gift certificate or trust me, Boisvert, next time they'll find somebody who will.

10,000 BC

(2008)

Directed by Roland Emmerich

I'm so glad they didn't call this "10,000 BCE". Who the hell decided that we couldn't use "BC" and "AD" anymore anyway? Probably some feminist.

These Conan-era pricks steal a caveman's woman, so he rounds up a posse to get her back. (Yes, the woman's wants and needs amount to approximately nil in this scenario, but it's fucking caveman times so cut them a break, ladies.) This mission, unfortunately, entails a *lot* of walking, maybe even more than the beginning of *Planet of the Apes* (1968) and all of *Stalker* (1979) combined. Walk walk walk. Walk walk walk. I got a stitch in my side just watching these assholes. Nevertheless, given my preference for prehistoric mammals over dinosaurs I figured that, if nothing else, the parts where they (finally) show up would be cool. Instead, all we get is one passable bird attack and a saber-toothed tiger that appears but doesn't do anything. Also it has stripes, which really bugs the shit out of me. I don't know why, but refuse to believe that saber-toothed tigers looked that much like regular-toothed tigers. And don't even get me started on the part where the saber-toothed tiger befriends our main guy. Is this a caveman movie or *Calvin & Hobbes*? It's all so fucking weak. And why why why why WHY is there a chick with a psychic link??? I swear, movies and books treat psychic links like they're as common as being left-handed but *there's no such things as psychic links, dammit, so you shouldn't just casually toss them into a story that's not specifically about psychic links.* God, Hollywood really pisses me off sometimes. Most of the time, actually.

Theodore Rex

(1995)

Directed by Jonathan Betuel

This intellect-raping whore of a movie, written and directed by a guy who generally churns out much more forgivably mediocre work (*My Science Project*, *The Last Starfighter*), is set in a future world shared by humans and humanoid dinosaurs, the latter having been reconstituted and evolved to us-like levels by our main bad guy, now hard at work on his *real* master plan: kick-starting a new ice age and then repopulating the world with animals of his choosing. And I think it's safe to assume that he'll select only "evil" animals like spider wasps and moray eels for this honor, while eliminating the lovable ones (koala bears, baby bunnies, dogs that can bark the alphabet) altogether. Supervillains. It's what we do.

So yeah, like *Tammy and the T-Rex* this is another "high concept" dinosaur movie pairing an intelligent dinosaur with a woman. But while *Tammy and the T-Rex* ladled on the gore and featured the scrumptious Denise Richards as the main chick, this movie wallows in slapstick idiocy like a pig wallows in its own vile filth and stars the obnoxious and hideous Whoopi Goldberg as the female cop forced to partner up with a clumsy humanoid dinosaur to solve the case. Also, Whoopi might be a robot (?) but this movie is so poorly written that I'm not entirely sure. Aiding the bad guy: a pack of red-eyed clones who apparently go to the same hair stylist as Whoopi, and, this movie's sole saving grace, Juliet Landau (AKA Drusilla from *Buffy the Vampire Slayer*), who. like chocolate, almost always makes everything better. Especially when you let it just melt in your mouth. Or, say, start dry-humping its leg. (Yeah, I know, my analogies tend to break down fairly quickly.) If nothing else, there is something charmingly surreal in watching Whoopi Goldberg (one of the ugliest woman on Earth) interact with Juliet Landau (arguably the hottest). A smarter villain would have foregone the tiresome Hugo Drax bullshit and simply cloned an army of Juliet Landaus for sale on the black market. Hell, I'd order a few myself. I could *easily* burn through three or four of those a year. More if they came with attachments.

(Just in case you think I'm being too hard on Whoopi, here's a 100% true story to set you straight: Back in the 1990s one of my ladyfriends called me in tears because some cat tried to pick her up at the grocery store by saying she looked like Whoopi Goldberg. "I don't look like Whoopi Goldberg, do I, Nigel?" I swear to God I'm not making this up. That's how repugnant Whoopi Goldberg is: just implying that you look like her is enough to make a grown woman cry.)

I shouldn't have to tell you that unfunny slapstick saturates this flick like old sperm saturates a hotel mattress ("...and then Theodore Rex's tail knocks something over." must appear on every page of the script), but it's actually structured like a buddy-cop movie, dutifully checking off every cliché in that beyond worn-out book and then clumsily mishandling every single one of them. Seriously, why propose such a left-field premise (dinosaurs living among us as equals) just to plug it into the laziest template possible, and fully *six years* after *Tango and Cash* brutally ass-raped that particular conceit into irrelevance by unapologetically being the dumbest possible example of it? Or at least the dumbest possible example where Tango isn't a talking dinosaur. Even if the whole thing wasn't wildly out of step with anything resembling Earthly concepts of entertainment, the sheer sloppiness on display is absolutely unforgivable. Take the countdown to the detonation of the ice age-inducing missile, for example: it's so wildly inconsistent that the only way it would make any sense is if the missile was flying through a time warp. Still, it's easy to understand why no one at the "keeping track of minutiae" level of this production could be bothered to care, because this flick was obviously doomed from day one, when Whoopi Goldberg decided that she didn't want to be in it (hey, I never said she was dumb) so they *legally forced her to*. Are you *fucking* killing me? That's like successfully dodging an assassin's bullet and then paying him to reload and shoot you point-blank in the face. *Theodore Rex* is filled with baffling exchanges that have the structure of jokes but make no real sense, and bewildering events regularly occur with no logical progression or set-up whatsoever. Why, at one point, are they suddenly flying around in a gyrocopter? Don't ask, because nobody knows. Even when an original idea does rear it's unwelcome head it's usually completely nonsensical. (Instead of fingerprints, dinosaurs have "tail prints", because... wait, what? Why? Seriously, just why?) And then, after all this, they have the nerve to pummel us with a heavy-handed "message" at the end, reminding us that we should "respect all species". Like this terrible fucking movie is going to finally convince me to stop kicking my dog. When they sued Rodney Dangerfield to force him to be in *Caddyshack II* you know what he did? He refused anyway and just coughed up the dough. You should have so much class, Whoopi Goldberg. Kiss my Jumpin' Jack ass.

Time of the Apes

(1987)

Directed by Atsuo Okunaka and Kiyo Sumi Fukazawa

Three nips (a woman and two children so annoying that even Gamera wouldn't associate with them) go into suspended animation and wake up on the Japanese version of the Planet of the Apes. The ape police chief – named (I swear to fucking God) "Gay Bar" – wants to kill them, but they escape and team up with an ape child and another human who's essentially the last man on Earth so I'll bet he's pretty happy to see our main chick, especially seeing as she's none too shabby. The pimp-ass leader of the apes (who's flashing some *mad* bling, including a medallion that appears to depict the Löwenbräu logo) goes against type by declaring that everyone should just get along, but Gay Bar has such a boner for man-murder that he initiates an ape civil war instead, which might've been a pretty cool development if we actually got to see any of it. Instead, we follow the humans, who are almost captured by the "bad" apes time and time again only to be aided and abetted by a mysterious UFO. Finally the "good" apes are declared the winners of this epic war they couldn't be bothered to show us, after which they let the humans follow the UFO over the mountains and, somehow, back to their normal time via some bullshit pseudo-scientific double-talk and you can suck it, *Time of the Apes*. This is pretty much the end of the line, all riders must exit, for people who have devoured all of the classic *Planet of the Apes* movies, TV shows, cartoons, comic books, and read-along LPs but still can't get enough of this shit. We're talking serious bottom-of-the-monkey-barrel here, but I'm not saying you *shouldn't* watch it. After all, where else are you gonna see an ape rolling around in a white-on-white trenchcoat suit, carrying a pimp cane, and sporting a goddamned Löwenbräu necklace?

Tomb of the Dragon

(2013)

Directed by Eric Styles

"Biologists will tell you that every living creature on the planet has been discovered..." declares the main guy at the beginning of this movie. Uh, no, that's like the last thing a biologist would say (besides "Being a biologist is a license to print pussy!", I suppose). Over 250 new birds, reptiles, and mammals were discovered in 2009 alone, the most recent date for which information was available on the first page of my Google search. And I'm pretty sure that of all people, a biologist would know this. No, what this movie is really saying here is "We were too lazy to do literally five seconds of research, but it doesn't matter because we're pretty sure that anyone who watches this movie is a moron anyway." To which I say: CHOKE TO DEATH ON COCK, creators of *Tomb of the Dragon*. Rest assured, if it wasn't my job I wouldn't watch your cunt movie or anything else you produced, ever, you condescending bags of shit. You can gargle my unwashed sack.

So, some assholes are trying to track down what they believe is a gigantic, unidentified bear. Well, they find it, and even though it's obviously a cartoon I love me some giant bears so the part where it unloads several metric tons of whoop-ass on these clowns did assuage my anger a little bit. Skip ahead to sometime later (though not *too* much later - apparently the lawsuits haven't even been settled yet) and the main guy is approached to track down another mysterious animal: a gigantic, previously unknown semi-aquatic reptile that's taken to killing people in broad daylight. Also known as a "dinosaur", at least where I come from (Ohio). Since there's no doubt that the creature exists, from here it basically plays out like a less annoying version of *Lake Placid* (1999), one without all the wink-wink nudge-nudge bullshit, and for a while it's not such a bad movie, despite its previously-noted disdain for us, the viewer. Unfortunately, it's only a matter of time before we get a good look at our dinosaur/lizard/monster and I'll take it from behind if it doesn't look like a giant-sized version of the goddamned Geico Gecko. Obviously seeing the universally-despised Geico Gecko gorily blown to pieces would be a cathartic crowd-pleaser, but as it turns out the monster isn't killed at the end so the design doesn't even have that going for it. And the whole "This is just the baby! The adult is still out there!" twist? That was already tired-ass bullshit back in 1983 when they broke it out for *Jaws 3*; it's also been used in *Gorgo* (1961), *The Beast* (1996), and *Gargantua* (1998).

Oh, and spoiler warning for like five different movies.

Triassic Attack

(2010)

Directed by Colin Ferguson

I'll cut this flick some slack regarding the rampaging dinosaur skeletons that a) are awful cartoon effects and b) roar even though they don't have vocal cords. Cartoons really are the only practical way to do walking skeletons, especially when you don't care how shitty your movie comes out anyway, and if I can buy them coming to life it's not too much of a stretch to buy that they can roar. But even after letting all that slide there's still:

- The frat guy who we're supposed to hate because he hazes people. Here's an example of his out-of-control behavior: he tells one pledge to do some push-ups, but then he says he's just kidding, the pledge doesn't really have to do the push-ups. Dying in gruesome horror is too good for this fiend.
- The nerd who's so tiresomely nerdy that it was just fucking embarrassing. For the writer, I mean, not the nerd.
- "That's utterly terrifying." You really have to see this part in context to fully understand, but believe me when I say that this is *literally* the worst line/pun to ever appear in any movie, book, TV show, or Bazooka Joe comic ever made. I have no doubt

whatsoever that future historians will identify "That's utterly terrifying." as the undisputed low point in the history of written language.

- The "happy" ending where everything works out just fine for the Native American Indian who intentionally and with malice brought the killer skeletons to life. Sure, he's directly responsible for the horrific slaughter of *at least* a dozen innocent people, most of them kids, but that's okay because the movie insists that he's one of the good guys. It's not like he was going around making people do push-ups or anything.

Seriously, do I even need to go on? The lacktalent "writer" who blew his way into this gig should be forced to eat a copy of this script once a week until the day he dies, because he deserves to spend the rest of his life shitting failure. As for the rest of this movie, well, the effects suck, the gore sucks, the action sucks, the jokes suck, the camerawork sucks, the sheriff's daughter in a bikini...

Okay, the sheriff's daughter in a bikini was pretty choice.

Turok: Son of Stone

(2008)

Directed by Curt Geda, Dan Riba, and Frank Squillace

Long, long before dinosaur-cowboy mash-ups like *The Valley of Gwangi* (see below) and *Jurassic ~~Cunt~~ Hunters* (see above) (or better yet, don't) came along there was a comic book whose entire mission statement was Indians vs. dinosaurs, and even though it only seemed to be sold at Sears in bagged packs of three where they always hid the shittiest comic in the middle so you couldn't identify it (it was usually *Woody Woodpecker*) enough people remembered it that over a decade later it inspired several new comics and novels, multiple video games, and a series of themed dick sheaths for all I know. Oh, and in 2008 this cartoon movie showed up, which is surprisingly violent and, somewhat less surprisingly, kinda stupid.

Two Indian tribes are having a gory little spat when a prehistoric terror bird unexpectedly horns in and decapitates one of their horses. Turns out there's an entire valley full of prehistoric whatnots located nearby, so some of the Indians investigate and after nearly being killed several times they discover more redskins living there, which is when our story completely derails because the next thing you know our main Injuns are running errands for the locals, collecting pterodactyl eggs and so forth, like they suddenly decided to take on all the side missions in an especially unfocused video game. Seriously, do your own shopping, assholes.

Now things just get embarrassing. Main guy Turok rides a pterodactyl around. The bad guy leads an army of out-of-shape cavemen sporting Stone Age beer bellies in an attack. After ruthlessly slaughtering everyone else, the bad guy, for absolutely no reason, keeps Turok alive long enough for Turok to escape and kill him. Turok rides *another* dinosaur around, because... they're already out of ideas, I guess? Honestly, minus the credits this movie is only 70 minutes long. Pretty sad, people. It's hard to believe that this 2008 production is actually cornier than the G-rated 1950s comic book that inspired it, but that said I suppose I've seen worse cartoons. (As long as Seth MacFarlane exists, there will always be worse cartoons.) And it's sure to be better than the proposed live-action movie, which, given his fondness for also-ran comic book characters, will almost certainly star Nicolas Cage.

Unknown Island

(1948)

Directed by Jack Bernhard

We're off to Dinosaur Island, and nothing's gonna derail this expedition! The only guy who's been there before won't sign up? Shanghai him! The crew decides to mutiny? Deliver a few beat-downs until they remember who's the boss! (It was Alyssa Milano. It was always Alyssa Milano.) The redhead putting up the cash is engaged to be married? Hit on her anyway! And you know how every adventure story features that one guy who endangers everybody by being especially selfish/cowardly/foolhardy/drunk/rapey, and in the end he finally gets what's coming to him? Well that's half the cast of this movie, so as you can imagine there are a few more hiccups along the way. Before it's all over they manage to lose their boat, burn down their own camp, and one clown even gets killed by a giant sloth! Are you fucking kidding me? Who gets killed by the goddamned *sloth?* What a bunch of rubes.

The Valley of Gwangi

(1969)

Directed by James O'Connolly

This traveling Wild West show is on its last legs, which is pretty pathetic seeing as the Wild West is still technically occurring when this movie takes place. They've got a new attraction sure to wow the slack-jawed masses though: the world's smallest horse, which turns out to be one of those prehistoric proto-horses just like the ones that famously got shitfaced on fermented grapes in that BBC documentary *Walking with Beasts*. Now Science is interested, and after the requisite skulduggery (involving gypsies, naturally) everyone descends into the hidden valley where the little horse came from only to find the place sick with fucking dinosaurs. Also, the salad dressing they make there is a game-changer. Sadly, very little time is actually spent in this mysterious valley (they're only there long enough to lose one guy); the rest of the movie concerns the Allosaurus they capture and unwisely put on display King Kong style, with similar results. Still, the Allosaurus does fight an elephant at one point, and gobbles up an evil midget (is there any other kind?), so that's kinda cool, I guess. After that it turns on the local Mexicans, who immediately hightail to the nearest church. I guess they think the Virgin Mary will save them, or maybe the patron saint of dinosaur attacks, whoever that is, exactly. (Probably St. Francis.) The dinosaur manages to get inside the church though (it's a big, Catholic one), so they lock it in there and burn the place to the ground, effectively eliminating two blights on their community for the price of one. The dinosaurs are realized via top-notch old-school special effects (even if the Allosaurus is obviously just a plastic toy during the cave-in scene); the main chick is a redhead (best of all heads); and there's two cowboys named "Bean" and "Rowdy" (because westerns are horrible). Mostly worth seeing.

Valley of the Dinosaurs

(1974)

Produced by Hanna-Barbera

Completely overshadowed by *Land of the Lost*, the *other* Saturday-morning dinosaur/Lost World series to premiere in the fall of 1974, *Valley of the Dinosaurs* didn't last very long, and watching it again it's easy to see why. The first episode is pretty wretched: a typical nuclear family, the Butlers, sucked via whirlpool into a world of prehistoric monsters, get themselves (and their inexplicably English-speaking caveman friends) into an absurdly convoluted bind and then solve the problem with applied science, adding an educational element to a cartoon that was crappy enough already. Too many subsequent episodes followed this same lazy pattern: the cave people are like "Don't do that shit," one of the "civilized" kids does it anyway, trouble ensues. Still, *Valley of the Dinosaurs* wasn't all bad: when she was actually drawn on-model (roughly 60% of the time, about average for Hanna-Barbera) teenage daughter Katie had a pretty nice ass (ladies, this would be a super-easy cosplay; someone please indulge me); the token comedic-relief pets (a dog named "Digger" and a baby stegosaurus named "Glump", which looks almost exactly like baby stegosaurus "Spike" from *The Land Before Time* not that I'm accusing them of stealing the design or anything but yes I am) weren't too odious; and they showcased a fairly wide range of prehistoric animals, finally straying away from the tiresome T-rex/Triceratops/Brontosaurus triumvirate that seemed to dominate dinosaur movies at the time. Subsequent episodes featured prehistoric ants, a mosasaur, a giant boar, an Ankylosaurus, a terror bird, and even giant, prehistoric camels, which I initially mocked until I looked it up and found out that they were a real thing. Unfortunately, cartoons in general were entering a period of extreme pussification at the time, so no one is gorily devoured, not even the annoying caveman extras who are constantly hovering in the background, openly doubting and complaining about everything the main characters do. Cartoons from this era rarely resolved their storylines, so the last we saw of the Butthole family they were still stranded in the Valley of the Dinosaurs. Methinks it might be time for a gritty, live-action Hollywood reboot featuring Kristen Stewart as the teenage daughter with the nice ass. Then again, after X number of rewrites it would probably end up being a fart comedy starring Kevin James so you know what, never mind.

Voyage to the Prehistoric Planet

(1965)

Directed by John Sebastian

Three rocketships are headed for Venus, but en route one of them is hit by a meteorite and explodes. "There is no fair or unfair. To a meteorite, you get hit, you die," one dude opines. What? Two guys and a really cool-looking old-school robot are sent down to the planet to scope shit out, but when they disappear three more cats are sent to look for them. Instead of the intelligent life they were probably hoping to find, team two is attacked by a giant plant, while team robot is attacked by primitive lizard men. The two teams also spy some dinosaurs and occasionally hear a woman singing, but nothing of consequence happens until team robot is trapped by a lava flow. The two guys order the robot to carry them through the lava, but it has a "self-preservation mechanism" so when they start to weigh it down it decides to throw them into the lava instead! Ha ha! It's a comedy of errors! As it turns out these two clowns are rescued in the nick of time, but the robot doesn't make it, prompting one guy to cry even though I don't recall him crying when a whole rocket full of actual human beings blew up at the beginning. Returning to their ship our crew flees as quickly as possible, after which it's revealed that there was intelligent life on Venus after all, which irrefutably proved itself by not making contact with these dumbasses.

Warbirds

(2008)

Directed by Kevin Gendreau

Dateline: World War Part 2. Some dames are flying a top secret mission over nip territory when a pterodactyl gets sucked into one of their engines and they crash on Dinosaur Island. Okay, I call bullshit. Oh, the existence of Dinosaur Island has been positively confirmed (cf. *Star-Spangled War Stories, Vol. 1*), and its historical significance can't be over-emphasized, but trusting an important military mission to bunch of broads? In 1945? Give me a fucking break. And since you can't kill dinosaurs by maxing out your credit card on shoes or "accidentally" getting pregnant you'd figure this would be a pretty short movie, but fortunately a man is actually in charge of this little clambake so a couple of people do manage to survive. You probably think I'm saying that just to be a dick, and I am, but apparently this movie agrees with me because despite all the "grrl power" posturing *almost every decision the chicks make turns out to be hilariously, disastrously wrong*. Seriously, this might be the most anti-chick pro-chick movie ever made. Let's see, what else is wrong with this flick? There's the "story", which is just a bunch of random tasks strung together video game style (Stage 1: Landing the Damaged B-29! Stage 2: Pterodactyl Dogfight! Stage 3: Obtaining the Fuel Barrels!). There's the lame cartoon airplanes. There's the HCDF Syndrome, of which it has a serious case. And, finally, there's the no tits. In short, not the Syphilis Channel's finest moment. Then again, what is?

When Dinosaurs Ruled the Earth

(1970)

Directed by Val Guest

Okay, hold on, back up the drink cart here. Am I understanding this right? Is the narrator trying to tell us that these cavemen sacrifice three hotties *every morning* to make the sun come up? You run out of pussy fast, perpetrating a scheme like that. Whatever the case, this time one of the hotties escapes, and she's quickly rescued by some sensible cavemen who know the value of a piece of ass in a lawless, no-rape-left-behind environment like caveman times or the Greek fraternity system. Later the cavemen who rescued her decide that they want to kill her too, but by this point the narrator is gone, long gone, check cashed at the bank it was drawn on and undoubtedly on his second beer, so there's no way we'll ever know what *their* problem is. Why? Because everyone else in this flick communicates in some sort of made-up caveman language, rendering every single line of dialogue completely incomprehensible and thus hilariously pointless. Which is especially moronic seeing as talking constitutes the vast majority of this movie. In fact, here's a rough breakdown of the elements that make up *When Dinosaurs Ruled the Earth*:

- People in their underwear spouting gibberish: 70%
- Cool-ass dinosaur effects: 15%
- Stone Age catfights: 1%
- Nipples accidentally slipping out of cavegirl costumes: < 1%
- Miscellaneous (walking around, freaking out, standing on a beach/staring at the sea): 14%

The creature effects are pretty kickass (I especially liked the giant crabs), so my suggestion is to hit fast-forward immediately and only slow it down for the dinosaur scenes. I guarantee you won't miss a single thing you'd actually care to see. Except maybe that nipple.

Where Time Began

(1977)

Directed by J. Piquer Simon

Music performed by "Clean Wheat"? What the hell kind of name is that? Not just for a band, for anything.

It certainly seems to take most of recorded time to get through this movie, which can't be bothered to start until the halfway point and spends that first half focused on four morons stumbling around in the dark, an apt metaphor for the production of this flick if I ever heard one. A map hidden in an old book leads to the entrance to the center of the Earth, which in the real world is filled with a delicious, nougaty molten center but in books and movies is always where God keeps his leftover dinosaurs. Our heroes hire a guide who insists on being paid in sheep (fucking pervert), and soon they're descending into an extinct volcano and successfully entering the depths of the Earth, although they do lose all of their drinking water *and* their guidebook along the way in unrelated, klutzy incidents. Maintaining this slapsticky tone: the token chick falls into quicksand; the leader of the expedition fires off a flare gun in a cave for no reason, triggering a cave-in; a clumsily-accessed torrent of water nearly knocks them off their feet; one guy falls and rolls down an incline; and so on and so forth. They really are fucking idiots. Somehow no one actually dies though, and they eventually reach a subterranean sea inhabited by dinosaurs (two of them!), which I prayed would eat the entire expedition, except maybe the chick, who if nothing else is at least passably bangable. It's all offensively family-friendly and slow as fuck, which means that the only real selling points are the dinosaurs: sure, they're basically puppets, but they have an undeniable (go ahead, try to deny it) old-school charm that you just don't get with special effects that are designed via computer or are actually good. From here our heroes are pursued by giant turtles (Only these clowns could be menaced by giant *turtles*. The real wonder is that they all manage to get away.), hassled by a monster gorilla, spot a few more dinosaurs (at a distance), and discover a secret high-tech laboratory manned by smug dicks from the future, before ultimately returning to the surface. "And thus ended our fantastic voyage!" says the narrator when it's (finally) all over. Oh, shut up.

The White Gorilla

(1945)

Directed by H.L. Fraser

"The jungle. Weird, mysterious..." And mostly stock footage, apparently. One night, a man stumbles out of the stock footage with a wild tale: he's seen a white gorilla, and... Er, okay, now he's apparently telling us about a silent movie he saw once. Seriously, what the fuck? It's obviously a silent movie, and he's just "watching" the action from the bushes! In pre-computer days this probably was a passable attempt to make it seem like our main guy was participating in what is obviously footage from a completely different (and much older) flick, but the inevitable result is to make him look like an enormous, unapologetic pussy who refuses to help out the silent movie dudes as they're captured by natives (while he hides in the bushes) and chased by lions (while he hides in a tree). It's a true celebration of cowardliness, and it's no wonder that he's hesitant to answer any questions about it, of which the cats he's telling it to have plenty, obviously. But nothing he's said or done up to now matters anyway, like at all, because suddenly the white gorilla shows up! Oh, wait, now the white gorilla is just wandering off again. Maybe he left the oven on or something. I guess that means there's time for another silent movie flashback, during which our main guy explains that while he was "tempted" to rescue a beautiful woman and a blind man from attacking lions he didn't because, you know, he might get hurt. Eventually the white gorilla, "sworn enemy of man", does drag some people off, probably to rape (male, female, no hole is *verboten* to the white gorilla), and at one point he half-heartedly fights another gorilla, but ultimately the bulk of this movie is the story of the most cowardly main guy in film history hiding in the bushes. Structurally, it's like watching someone else watch a movie, which come to think of it is exactly what's happening here. If I'd paid good, cash money to see this back in the day I would've been so pissed I probably would've burned the theater down. Hell, I watched it for free on the Internet and I still feel kind of ripped off. (It's in the public domain; don't get your willies in a dither, MPAA). In the end our main guy actually comes out of hiding long enough to shoot the white gorilla, while most of the other characters are simply declared dead with a dismissive wave of the hand and/or completely forgotten.

Another winner from the Golden Age of Hollywood.

White Pongo

(1945)

Directed by Sam Newfield

I guess 1945 was the year of the white gorilla, further driven home when a bunch of white dudes in white suits insist that *this* white gorilla could be "the most amazing anthropological discovery of the century". I'll bet that if, instead of black & white, they could've made this movie in just "white", they would've done it.

An expedition sets out to find the white gorilla, but as it turns out there's a whole tribe of (regular) gorillas out there, guarding (in the loosest sense of the term) a fabulous treasure, making this movie a sort of proto-*Congo*. Or "Pongo", if you will. This expedition doesn't fight the gorillas though, and no one gets the treasure. In fact, nothing of import really happens at all, the directionless story content to ramble around in that go-nowhere manner seemingly exclusive to also-ran 1940s movies. It's the type of old movie most reviewers would call "tepid" (because people who watch old movies don't like to say "sucks ass"), and it's uptight even by pussified 1945 standards. "How dare you, you insolent young bounder!" is the most one guy can muster when he learns that someone wants to make his daughter into a rape-slave. It's also racist (their black guide is named "Mumbo Jumbo"), and as far as I can tell the biggest name in the cast is the cafe owner from *I Accuse My Parents* (1944), playing the remarkably non-odious comedic relief. Still, at least this is a real movie, not some Mad Libs charm quilt stitched together from whatever the producers found in an overlooked dumpster behind the old silent film lot. In a perfect world, someone would have paired this up with *The White Gorilla* and re-released them in the 1970s as a "Honky Monkey Double Feature". But clearly this is not a perfect world, as evidenced by the fact that casting a voodoo spell on a stolen lock of Fiona Apple's hair and then swallowing it doesn't actually make her fall in love with you. I think it might've turned her into a zombie though. My bad on that one.

Yor: The Hunter from the Future

(1983)

Directed by Anthony M. Dawson

You're the hunter from the future! Choose from 16 possible endings.

This movie is about Yor, a remarkably GQ caveman who's here to fight dinosaurs and score hot pussy, and he's all out of neither. At one point these other guys steal some of his pussy, so he kills a giant bat and uses it to hang-glide into their cave so he can kick the shit out of them and get it back. That's how dedicated this man is to pussy. That's not to say he doesn't have other interests though. If he lived in modern times, those interests would probably include the gym and telling everyone how many reps he did at the gym. There aren't many gyms in caveman times though (and the few they do have only provide free weights, no machines), so instead he's become fixated on this necklace he wears, which he's convinced has some greater significance, probably because it's shiny. In an effort to learn more he journeys to this mysterious island on the recommendation of one of his bitches, but once there he's attacked by robots because – surprise! – it's not the prehistoric, free-weight past after all, it's actually the post-elliptical future! I assume this was meant to be a shocking twist, but seeing as it's right there in the title (*Planet of the Apes*) the effect is underwhelming, to say the least. That misstep aside, this sounds like it could be a pretty decent movie, but don't be fooled. The gore is strictly PG-level and despite Yor's obsession with pussy there's no tits either. It's hard to believe that a movie based on such a solid three-pronged premise (dinosaurs + robots + hot chicks) could suck this hard, but it does so the only possible explanation is that the people making it either didn't care at all, or were actively trying to sabotage it. As proof, I will come up with an infinitely better version of *Yor: The Hunter from the Future* in like two seconds. The following synopsis is entirely off the top of my head, and edited only for typos:

Part 1: Pimp-ass caveman Yor is hanging out with his friends when a dinosaur appears, slaughters the shit out of everybody, and starts eating them, gorily tearing the bodies to pieces and choking the pieces down in the most repulsive manner imaginable. A few sexy cavegirls do manage to escape, but in the process most of their clothes are torn off. Yor grabs a spear and hurls it right into the dinosaur's eye, causing blood to fountain out of the eye socket and soak down all of the surviving chicks in a grisly approximation of a wet T-shirt contest. Dead as fuck, the dinosaur topples over, landing on an unlucky cavegirl and gorily squashing her flat. The dust slowly settles and then, after a slight pause for dramatic effect, one of the surviving cavegirls pukes.

Part 2: The remaining cavegirls are so happy to be alive that they all start twerking. Then, to show Yor their appreciation, they take turns fucking him. He can only service so many girls at a time though, so while the others are waiting they dyke out with each other. As the centerpiece of the movie, this scene will go on for about forty minutes.

Part 3: Holy shit! In an M. Night Shyamabantha-kappadeltagammalan style twist, it turns out that it's not the caveman era after all, it's the future! (To further obfuscate this, the title will be changed to "Yor: The Hunter from a Distant Age That's Totally Not the Future"). Robots sporting semi-functional metallic penises swoop in and start raping the chicks. (Why would anyone build a robot with a semi-functional penis, you ask? Clearly you've never attended supervillain school.) Now Yor's really forced to bust some heads, caving in robot skulls left and right with the many stone axes that are laying around. (Why are there a bunch of stone axes just laying around? Because it's caveman times. Duh.) All this racket wakes up another dinosaur that comes rolling in and starts furiously crushing and/or eating everything, robots included, so the robots are forced to engage it in an epic battle, finally blowing it to pieces. Blood, guts. chunks of dinosaur meat, half-digested cavegirls, and mangled robot parts rain down all over everybody.

Part 4: Yor thinks it's all over, but – Ha! – fat chance: there's one robot left and Yor's all out of stone axes so he has to fight it with his bare hands. Yor and the robot beat the absolute shit out of each other while the theme from *Rocky* plays, until Yor finally tears the robot's electronic heart out in a shower of sparks. "Please. Only. Now. Do. I. Know. What. It. Means. To. Be. Human," the robot begs. "Now you know what it means to be DEAD!" says Yor and shoves its robot heart down its robot throat. Then it explodes spectacularly, like someone dropped an H-bomb on the Death Star, but leaving Yor unharmed due to some clever editing. There's only one cavegirl left, played by Avril Lavigne. She smiles and shows Yor her flawless rack, but when he steps towards her she suddenly fast-draws two six-shooters and puts him down because – super double twist – it's *really* Wild West days! Then she just stands there, naked, so we have something to look at while the credits roll. The end.

Now *that* would've been an instant classic. Are you taking notes, Hollywood?

The Greatest Adventure

(1929)

A novel by John ~~Taint~~ Taine

Some people just don't write good. Writing isn't about how "literary" the final result sounds, it's about crafting a story that people want to read, and that's impossible when that story is told via clunky, convoluted sentences pepper-sprayed with unnecessary 25-cent words. Here's an example:

"There's your immortal whale, Captain," the doctor sobbed when from very emptiness he ceased his calisthenics.

An efficient writer, one who wasn't desperately grasping for validation, wouldn't break out some clumsy-ass shit like "when from very emptiness he ceased his calisthenics". He would've simply said "after he puked". And that's a linchpin example since puking is so central to this novel. It starts out like any other Lost World adventure, with a bunch of unlikable dickholes fucking off to the Antarctic to look for the hordes of (recently) deceased dinosaurs these salty, crusty seamen supposedly discovered. When they locate the dinosaurs though – dead as hell and decomposing on the beach – something's not quite right: they seem less like actual dinosaurs than like imperfect copies, like this is the place where Jurassic Park dumps all its rejects or something.

After lots of boring speeches and theorizing the mystery is finally solved, but it's hardly a satisfying reveal seeing as the characters in this book have, from the first, constantly kept each other in the dark regarding important developments for no other reason than a clumsy attempt to generate fake suspense. This never works of course, unless you find it nail-biting when your friends needlessly withhold pertinent information from you. In which case it's probably a Hitchcockian adventure every time you have a big piece of spinach stuck in your teeth. Along the way our main crew spends a LOT of time dicking around with rotting dinosaur carcasses and blowing them up with TNT to see what's inside, leading to repeated descriptions of the rank-ass stench and much subsequent vomiting. The surviving dinosaurs, meanwhile, have taken to scavenging in repulsive piles of their own putrefying dead in a gigantic cavern that basically amounts to a prehistoric charnel house. There's also a scene where a dinosaur has everyone barricaded inside a tunnel so they blow its head off with dynamite...

In their confusion they blundered directly into the headless stump of neck–gushing blood like a hydrant.

...and then proceed to explode their way through the headless corpse to get to the other side:

When the gory job was done they were scarlet from boots to hair.

Other dinosaurs are "trampled to smears" by their brethren or "roasted alive" and then explode in midair, their "steaming viscera" raining from the sky. It's basically dinosaur gore porn.

Frankly there are any number of better Lost World/dinosaur novels out there, including Edgar "Rice" Burroughs' *Caspak* trilogy and even Lin Carter's *Zanthodon* series (which also features pirates, because Lin Carter is apparently ten years old), but for sheer baldfaced repulsiveness, *The Greatest Adventure*, as boring and badly-written as it is, has all of them beat. If you consider that a recommendation, I'd say the two of us are definitely on the same wavelength.

Don't miss out!

Visit the website below and you can sign up to receive emails whenever Mr. Satanism publishes a new book. There's no charge and no obligation.

https://books2read.com/r/B-A-TCXC-NBLJ

BOOKS 2 READ

Connecting independent readers to independent writers.

Also by Mr. Satanism

66.6 Absurd Movies About the Devil
Legendary House of Haunted Hell
Trash of the Titans
Night of the Living Dud
Lifetime Movies... for Men
Shark Weak: The Worst Shark Movies Ever Made
The Not-At-All-Cleverly-Titled Book of Dragon Movies
Snakes, Rats, Spiders, and Bats: A Creepy-Crawly Movie
Compendium
Monkeys & Dinosaurs: Cinema as High Art, Vol. 1
Hex Crimes: The Worst Witch Movies Ever Made
Close Encounters of the Worst Kind
Triskaidekaphilia - Mr. Satanism's 13th Book
Vampire Movies Suck
Werewolves Don't Eat Brunch
Mr. Satanism's Invisible Book
A Yeti Brew (And Bigfoot Too)
The Magical Golden Rainbow Book of Crappy Wizard of
Oz Movies
Cannibal Attraction
A Chronology on Elm Street
Mr. Satanism Puts Down Your Favorite Dog (...Movies)
A Collection of Woke Movie Reviews